THE MALTESE

Diminutive Aristocrat

VICKI ABBOTT

 HOWELL BOOK HOUSE
NEW YORK

Howell Book House
IDG Books Worldwide, Inc.
An International Data Group Company
919 E. Hillsdale Boulevard
Suite 400
Foster City, CA 94404

For general information on IDG Books Worldwide's books in the U.S., please call our Consumer Customer Service department at 800-762-2974. For reseller information, including discounts and premium sales, please call our Reseller Customer Service department at 800-434-3422.

Library of Congress Cataloging-in-Publication Data available upon request.

ISBN: 1-58245-160-5

Manufactured in the United States of America

10 9 8 7 6 5 4 3 2 1

Cover and book design by George J. McKeon

Dedication

This book is dedicated to anyone who ever owned a dog and had a dream.

To my husband, Larry, whose love and support have enabled me to turn my dreams in this sport into reality. To my two wonderful daughters, Aubrey and Tara, who have always considered their mother's involvement in the sport of dogs more of an asset than a liability. To the memory of our friend, Frank Oberstar, and his unforgettable contribution to Maltese as a breeder, exhibitor and judge.

And to the Maltese breeders throughout the world, whose dedication makes the future very bright for this breed.

Larry and Vicki Abbott and Ch. Shanlyn's Rais'n A Raucous.

Acknowledgments

I wish to thank the many Maltese breeders and owners in this country who have never said no when I needed something for this book. Had I not taken on this project, I might never have learned so much more about them all and their wonderful little dogs! I only wish there had been more hours in each day, as from every conversation I added to my knowledge of this breed from their experiences.

There are many beautiful pictures in this book, and I am truly grateful for those who have gone to great lengths to send me these treasured photographs depicting the wonderful personality of the Maltese breed. It is sometimes very difficult to produce a good photograph of a white dog, so my appreciation also goes to the photographers who have caught these little guys at their best! A Maltese definitely has greeting card appeal, to say the least.

Special thanks go to The American Maltese Association and its Education Committee for their permission to use a few of the illustrations from their wonderful *Illustrated Guide to the Maltese Standard,* Amy Fernandez, illustrator. If you would care to have the whole booklet, you can obtain one by contacting the committee at the address posted in Appendix A.

I would also like to thank all of the special owners and breeders of the Maltese that Larry and I have campaigned. Your trust and support not only enabled all of us to achieve our goals, but also brought national attention to this breed for years to come and paved the way for others that followed. Thanks to Elsie Burke (breeder and owner of Ch. Louan's Apache Starfire); Marjorie Lewis (breeder), Mariko Sukezaki and David and Sharon Newcomb (owners of Ch. Melodylane Sing's O' Al-Mar Luv); Lynda Podgurski (breeder), Joseph Joly and David and Sharon Newcomb (co-owners of Ch. Shanlyn's Rais'n A Raucous with me); the late Carol Frances

Andersen (breeder and owner of Ch. Sand Island Small Kraft Lite); and our friend Jere Olson (who was Carol's right hand and *Henry's* very best friend). The experiences that we had and the knowledge that we gained while showing these dogs cannot be measured—we loved them all.

And finally, I would like to express my appreciation to my husband Larry, who, for many years, not only planned every step of each dog's career, but also traveled along with me to make sure everything went smoothly. In addition to that, while I've been working on this book, he has taken care of the dogs, made the meals, done the laundry, and stayed up late at night with me so that I could finish on time!

Contents

(Vicki Abbott and Ch. Sand Island Small Kraft Lite, Henry)

Introduction

There is one book in my library that I will never part with. It has no monetary value, but stands for the beginning of a very long career in dogs. It is a worn and faded paperback, and the pages have long since yellowed—it is over 40 years old. The book is *Champion Dog Prince Tom*, by Jean Fritz and Tom Clute. It is the Cinderella story of a small, skinny Cocker Spaniel puppy—the runt of the litter—who ended up being one of the greatest Obedience and Field Trial Champions of his time. It made me believe that anything is possible in the sport of dogs if you set your goals high and expect to work to get there. It also made me realize what a little dog with a big heart is capable of.

While I read that book in the early years of elementary school, my belief in these things has never changed, mostly because of the dogs I have had the privilege to know and love—a great many of them being Maltese. After having owned a number of different breeds—Collies, Poodles, Miniature Schnauzers and Pekingese—I was attracted by the beauty and elegance of the Maltese. I had found the breed to set my goals with.

My success in the show ring has been exciting, to say the least. Over the years, I have bred and finished numerous Maltese Champions under the Scylla prefix. In 1985, I handled a little dog that I had bred, Best in Show Champion Scylla's Mina Maya Starfire. Starfire became known around the world, and was the #1 Maltese in 1985. Since that time, until my retirement from professional handling in 1995, I had the honor of handling some of the nation's top Maltese (Best in Show Champion Louan's Apache Starfire—#1 Maltese in 1988, Best in Show Champion Melodylane Sings O' Al-Mar Luv—#1 Maltese 1992–1993, Best in Show Champion Shanlyn's Rais'n A Raucous—#1 Maltese and #1 Toy Dog 1994, and Best in Show Champion Sand Island Small

Kraft Lite, the top winning Maltese Dog of all time, affectionately known as *Henry*). In Henry, we had finally found our *Champion Dog Prince Tom*, as he was definitely not the pick of his breeder Carol Andersen's litter, yet his accomplishments will go down in history. The highlight of my years in the sport of dogs came when Henry and I won the Toy Group at Westminster Kennel Club.

Early in my endeavors with the Maltese breed, I became involved with the parent club, The American Maltese Association. I became the AMA Recording Secretary in 1981 and served in that capacity for 17 years. I was also appointed the chairman of the AMA Maltese Video committee, and, with two other dedicated breeders, was proud to help produce the official AKC Maltese Video. As past and current chairman of the AMA Education committee, I am serving with a group of long-time breeders of Maltese to mentor and help breeders and judges to gain more knowledge about the Maltese breed standard.

It has been very rewarding during my career to have been honored by my peers with two very personal awards. In 1988 I was honored with the American Maltese Association Outstanding Member Award, and in 1992 with the Kennel Review Award for Best New Female Professional Handler.

This book is intended to assist anyone who owns, or is considering the possibility of owning a Maltese. It is our hope that every Maltese owner will be educated in responsible pet ownership for the welfare of this beautiful breed, thereby reducing the need for Maltese rescue. While it might seem like a wonderful idea to get that cute, white, fluffy puppy for Christmas, or a surprise birthday present, adding a dog to your life should be a well thought out process commenced at a time when he can have your undivided attention.

There is nothing in the world that can compare to owning a Maltese, whether it is a top-winning AKC Champion, or the champion mischief maker of the family. It will become obvious to you, as you read this book, that a little Maltese is capable of very big accomplishments. A favorite saying of breeders is that "A Maltese is a big dog in a little body."

I have to add to that and say, "With a *very* big heart."

VICKI ABBOTT, NOVEMBER 1, 1999

(Photo by Pamela McDonald)

CHAPTER ONE

For Love of a Little White Dog

Perhaps as a child you saw him in the window at a department store—the plush stuffed animal with the long white hair, bows in appropriate places, a brush tied around his neck for grooming. Or maybe you were enthralled by the real one you recently saw in the lady's bag (with his head sticking just out of the top) at the mall. Or you've stopped to get gas, you look to the left, and lo and behold, there's the cutest little thing barking at you from the headrest of another car! Warning—a Maltese in any form can be addictive at first sight!

A LOOK BACK

Throughout history, Maltese have had a profound effect on all who have encountered them. The breed is thought to have originated on the small island of Malta, a trading center located in the Mediterranean Sea. They became world travelers; from Malta, the little white dogs were transported to the East and West over sea and land by their owners, eventually leading them to become treasures for royalty and valuable for trade. We know that these little lap dogs existed as far back as ancient Greece because Maltese are found on Greek vases dated about 500 B.C. as well as appearing in Greek texts with stories of their

A Maltese puppy is irresistible! (Photo by S. Kenner & C. Pearson)

extraordinary attachments to their masters and their masters' tributes to them. That seems to be the theme throughout history—from Egypt 600 to 300 B.C., where evidence can be found that the Maltese were worshipped, to the present day where tales are still heard of this little dog's great devotion to his master.

WHAT BREED IS THAT? I WANT ONE!

So you've seen this little ball of white hair with the big black eyes and nose and you're hooked. How can you get one of them? Considering the ideal—that purchasing a puppy is a lifetime

The Maltese has been bred through the years to be a dedicated companion. (Photo by Rosemarie Saccardi)

Genki is a typical Maltese puppy with lots of energy and curiosity! (Photo by Mariko Sukezaki)

investment—let's consider *need* versus *want*. You *want* a Maltese because, well, how could you resist? He's so cute with that long white hair! He is energetic and outgoing, seems to love people and is so small he certainly couldn't eat very much!

But does this breed meet your *needs* for a companion animal? And can you meet his? Understanding what breed of dog would best fit into your particular lifestyle can save a lot of agony and can reward you with a wonderful lifetime relationship with your dog.

A LITTLE GOES A LONG WAY

If space is an issue in deciding on the perfect breed of dog for you, consider a Maltese.

You can walk the streets of New York and find a Maltese on a lead on almost any block. The reason for this is that they make most excellent apartment dogs requiring less room than a larger breed. They do need exercise on a daily basis, but they are not prone to knocking over your knick-knacks with their tails! On the other hand, they also make excellent house pets for people with a little larger

home. A fenced-in yard is a must if you are going to let your valuable pet out in the backyard, however, because a small Maltese can get himself into a lot of trouble if let loose. There also have been instances of dogs being snatched from the backyard of their owners if left unwatched. Maltese are a very flashy breed and will attract quite a bit of attention.

The Maltese standard calls for a dog under 7 pounds, with 4 to 6 pounds preferred for the show ring. When reputable breeders who are breeding for show-quality animals have a puppy in the litter that does not meet their size requirements, they may decide to sell him as a pet. This does not mean you will get a deficient animal. In fact, it may mean you got lucky and will be able to purchase a top-quality Maltese as a pet just because he is a little over or under the size that the breeder wants for the show ring!

The small size of a Maltese has advantages. If you travel by automobile, your little dog can travel safely in a small crate with you, and many motels will accept only small dogs.

If you travel by plane, your Maltese can travel in a crate under the seat in front of you

Having Maltese in your home does not demand a lot of space. (Photo by Mariko Sukezaki)

A Maltese enjoys every bit of the attention he attracts! (Photo by Andrea Noel)

on most major airlines with a reservation in advance. A Maltese can fit in your lap comfortably and in your bed without taking up too much room (and these dogs definitely think they belong in your bed!). This breed is an excellent choice for someone who is looking for a small, portable companion with a sweet temperament.

LIFESTYLES OF THE SMALL YET DEMANDING

Because of his size, a Maltese often is mistakenly thought of as a frail breed. Although small, he is a hardy dog. Generally, Maltese as a breed are not prone to any particular illnesses, especially if obtained from a responsible breeder. The Maltese does not consider his small stature when he proudly lets something three or four times his siz know that it has invaded his space! If other dogs live in the household where you are planning to raise your puppy, realize that, although a Maltese is friendly and will usually get along with about any breed of dog, care must be taken for his safety.

The older or larger dog might be overbearing in play or might actually feel threatened by the new member of the family. A Maltese will make a wonderful addition to families with children as long as the children are supervised and are old enough to understand the care of a small dog. Extreme injury can occur to a puppy if dropped or squeezed, so if very young children are part of the family, it

This breed can go anywhere with you—it's the portable pet! (Photo by Catherine Lawrence)

Keep a watchful eye out when your small Maltese decides to let a bigger dog know who's boss. (Photo by Judy Crowe)

Although a young Maltese will be good with children, supervision is a must for the safety of the puppy. (Photo by Andrea Noel)

might be advisable to wait until they are a little older or choose a larger breed of dog.

The Maltese is a lap dog, a guard dog and a playmate rolled into one little animal. He will be content to lie in your lap for hours or to sit and watch your favorite television program with you (and they do watch). A Maltese will not bark incessantly at any old thing; rather, he will let you know if the doorbell rings, the phone rings, the smoke alarm goes off or someone strange is approaching, even a long distance away that you might not see or hear! A Maltese will entertain himself if you do not—he is playful and inquisitive and will always find something of interest. You will laugh as you watch the many antics of this breed. A Maltese will demand your attention— you cannot ignore him. Maltese are perpetual puppies even into old age!

TEA FOR TWO

If companionship is what you want, you are looking in the right place. Above all, a Maltese is a companion animal. It is their purpose and what they are bred to do. Enough cannot be said about obtaining a puppy from a responsible breeder who will be breeding for that lovely temperament that says Maltese. They are sweet tempered, want to please and are not overly aggressive or mean in any way.

Many stories have been passed down through the ages about Maltese lying by the sides of their sick masters aiding in their recovery. They seem to know when their person is not happy or well. They share in your excitement—we have a little

All wrapped up and ready to go! (Photo by M. Martin)

dog who is always invited to the NBA finals party because he jumps up and down and barks when the home team scores a basket! They are characters and they are clowns, but what they want most of all is to be with you. They simply do not fare well if left out in the backyard because they basically are not outside dogs.

If your lifestyle takes you away from home a majority of the time, this breed is not for you. This does not mean you cannot provide for a Maltese if you work. It only means that you must find some good, quality time on a consistent basis. Time spent with your Maltese will bring many rewards, and you will have a dedicated little friend!

CROWNING GLORY

It is said that the beautiful Maltese coat is his crowning glory. When deciding on a Maltese as your companion, the grooming aspect of the relationship and the time it will involve should be a consideration. You must be prepared to keep your friend's coat healthy and unmatted with daily brushing as well as having an overall bathing and grooming routine. The Maltese coat can be kept long and silky or can be kept in a short puppy cut; either way, you must be willing to invest the time. Many a poor little Maltese has ended up without a home and in a shelter for the same reason he was purchased—his beautiful white hair. This is every good breeder's nightmare. Although it is a learning process, the

The sweet expression on this puppy is indicative of typical Maltese attitude. (Photo by S. Kenner & C. Pearson)

The luxurious coat of the Maltese, as seen here on Ch. Crisandra's Petit Point Lace, requires a certain amount of care. Consider this responsibility before deciding on this breed. (Photo by S. Kenner & C. Pearson)

dedicated owner can indeed take care of the grooming of his own Maltese. The breeder from which the puppy is purchased should be willing to assist with this. Many publications are available with instructions on how to care for the Maltese coat, and some are listed in the Bibliography section in the back of the book.

Ch. Aennchen's Poona Dancer. (Photo by F. Oberstar & L. Ward)

CHAPTER TWO

A History of the Maltese

Melitaie was the ancient name for the island of Malta. Evidence suggests that a great civilization exist-ed there even before Malta was settled by the Phoenicians around 1500 B.C. Located in the mid-dle of the Mediterranean Sea, this small ancient island grew to become one of the most prosperous and celebrated societies in the then-known world because of its strategic location for trade. It is said that the *Melitaie Dog*, the name given to the Maltese by the Greeks and Romans, was transported from this island to many other parts of the world.

The Melitaie Dog is pictured on ancient Egyptian artifacts and Greek vases and is recorded in ancient poetry, serving as evidence that the dogs were considered quite valuable. They were held in high esteem by their owners, and many were presented as gifts for royalty. It is recorded that the Roman Emperor Claudius was the owner of a Maltese, as was Publius, the Roman governor of Malta. Records also show that, from the East, Maltese were kept by Sultans of the Turkish Empire, and they are documented as hav-ing been in the royal courts as far east as China. They were exalted in art and literature throughout the centuries, even on into the Renaissance in France, Spain and Italy.

Although it is known that Maltese arrived in England around 1509—during the reign of King Henry VIII—they did not become widely recognized in that area until his daughter, Elizabeth I, received one as a gift from the Sultan of Turkey. During this time, it was widely believed that Maltese actually held medicinal powers and were able to draw pain and illness out of their owners. They were placed under the bedcovers, positioned where the pain or illness had occurred in hopes of a cure. This, in addition to the

B.A. Hyland, Maltese Terrier, *oil on canvas, 1881, from the collection of Richard D. Hammond.*

R. Monunt, Maltese and English Toy Spaniel, *oil on canvas, 1890, from the collection of Richard D. Hammond.*

breed's loving and devoted nature, was obviously the reason why the Maltese received the nickname of "comforter."

Throughout the following centuries in England, the existence of these small dogs was fairly well documented in art and literature, and in the nineteenth century, interest in the Maltese as a purebred animal was established.

The first available information about the breeding or showing of Maltese goes back to 1862, at which time twenty Maltese were entered in the Holborn show in London and forty-one in the Islington show. Mr. Robert Mandeville, regarded as the most outstanding Maltese breeder of that time, won first and second prizes with his dogs, Mick and Fido. It was from this time to the early 1900s that the purebred Maltese obtained its greatest level of popularity and began to be exported to the United States and Canada.

THE MALTESE IN AMERICA

The Maltese breed within the United States had its ups and downs from about 1888 (when the first Maltese were entered into the American Kennel Club [AKC] stud book) until the 1950s. The two Maltese who were the first to be registered were Snips and Topsy, both of unknown pedigree. Apparently, thirteen years then went by before another two Maltese were registered. In 1902 there were six, and the number steadily increased until 1918. Then the registration of the breed steadily decreased—almost to extinction in the United

England-Ch. Vicbrita Pimpfernel, bred by Mrs. M. White. (Photo by F. Oberstar & L. Ward)

Ch. Invicta Leckhampton Cinderella, owned by Frank Oberstar and Larry Ward, was an English import from Miss Neame and Mrs. Brierly. (Photo by L. Ward & F. Oberstar)

States by 1939. By the year 1951, the number had gradually grown again, and the AKC registrations totaled 1,240. The breed's popularity then started to increase dramatically. In 1970, more than 4,000 Maltese were registered; since that time, the numbers have increased steadily as has the popularity of the Maltese among breeders and pet owners.

Early Influences

Registrations in the AKC stud book evidently were originally made on the basis of show wins. The first Maltese champion recorded by the American Kennel Club was Thackery Rob Roy, whelped in 1901 and owned by Mrs. C. S. Young.

In 1902, out of six registrations, five were owned by a Mr. W. P. Farmer of Chicago, Illinois. Mr. Farmer (Union Park Kennels) imported his foundation stock from Europe and eventually sold his Maltese to breeders in the United States, helping them to establish their own breeding programs. Other renowned Maltese breeders during this time period were Miss Josie Newman (Travilla Kennels, Missouri) and Mrs. Gertrude Ross Phalen (Rossmore Kennels, Illinois). Mrs. Phalen is known to have shown one of the smallest studs in the country at the time. The Maltese during this time period were mostly at the top of the standard—6 or 7 pounds. Mrs. Phalen's Ch. Sonny Boy was just $3^1/4$ pounds!

It seemed as though the breed was on its way in the United States, and Maltese breeders continued to dedicate themselves to produce better

Imported from England and bred by Mrs. M. White, Vicbrita White Rose at 10 weeks old. (Photo by F. Oberstar & L. Ward)

and better specimens of the breed. Many breeders imported dogs from Great Britain, Canada, Germany, France and Italy to improve their lines.

In the 1930s, however, something would happen that would almost destroy the future of the Maltese breed in this country. The steady decline of the breed after 1930 has been attributed to the outbreak of distemper before there were adequate immunizations for the disease. Evidently many dogs were lost, leading to the near extinction of most Maltese kennels and very nearly the breed in the United States.

Persistence Pays Off

The few Maltese breeders who were left heroically set out to re-establish the breed in the United Sates and Canada. In the 1940s and 1950s, two Maltese kennels were very instrumental in increasing the popularity of the Maltese breed—Villa Malta (Massachusetts) and Aennchen (New Jersey). Dr. Vincenzo Calvaresi started his breeding program in the late 1930s. His Villa Malta Kennels finished more than 100 champions, not the least of which was Ch. Ricco of Villa Malta, the sire of forty-one champions. Dr. Calvaresi's breeding program not only was one of quantity but one of quality, and a great number of the top winning showdogs of today can trace their past to the original Villa Malta Kennels. Mr. Calvaresi showed many strikingly beautiful dogs including braces and teams he campaigned from coast to coast. He was quite a showman and presented his dogs with such flair that it drew attention to the breed that had never before been experienced. Many dedicated breeders came to Villa Malta to buy breeding stock; one of these breeders was Mrs. Virginia T. Leitch of Jon Vir Kennels. Mrs. Leitch not only purchased foundation stock from Villa Malta Kennel, she also imported Maltese to compliment her breeding program, which became very highly regarded.

Aennchen Antonelli (right) with one of her group-winning Maltese. (Photo by L. Ward & F. Oberstar)

In the mid-1950s, Tony and Aennchen Antonelli (Aennchen Maltese) received their first brood bitch from Virginia Leitch of Jon Vir fame. The bitch, Aennchen's Jon Vir Royal Gopi, produced the Antonellis' first top-producing champion dam, Champion Aennchen's Puja Dancer MMA (Maltese Merit Award). Puja took Best of Winners at the Westminster Dog Show in New York in 1956. Among the champions Puja produced were

two full brothers, American Bermuda Champion Aennchen's Siva Dancer MMA and Champion Aennchen's Shikar Dancer MMA. Shikar won Best of Breed at Westminster in 1963 and was awarded five Best In Shows. Both were very influential studs and were the sires of many outstanding get that would have an influence on the breed for years to come.

For the Records . . . 1960s to 1980s

A Shikar Dancer daughter was the first Maltese purchased by Mr. Stimmler of Pennsylvania for his children Anna Marie and Gene. The lovely little girl was Ch. Co Ca He's Aennchen Toy Dancer. In 1964, Toy made her place in history by becoming the first Maltese to win the Toy Group at Westminster Kennel Club. This was quite an accomplishment at both ends of the lead because Anna Marie was 15 years old at the time. Toy also was the first Best of Breed Winner at an American Maltese Association National Specialty in 1966.

In February 1964, a female puppy chosen from a litter out of Siva Dancer would illuminate the pathway for all Maltese to come in the Toy ring. Ch. Aennchen's Poona Dancer, owned by Frank Oberstar and Larry Ward from Ohio, won 38 Best in Shows and 131 Group Firsts during her illustrious career, setting a record for Maltese. The breed had reached its pinnacle of recognition. Frank, Larry and Poona were a team that remains unsurpassed in this century. In 1966, Poona pranced to the top spot in the Toy Group at Westminster, making her only the second Maltese in history to do so. She won the 1967 and 1968 American

From left to right, Tony Antonelli, Lary Ward, Frank Oberstar and Aennchen Antonelli with
Ch. Aennchen's Poona Dancer. (Photo by William Kelly)

Maltese Association National Specialties and was the first Maltese to be presented the Quaker Oats Award for Top Group Winning Toy Dog (1967). Poona was retired in 1968 upon winning the first Best in Show for a Maltese that year.

History again was made when, three years in a row (1969, 1970 and 1971), the American Maltese Association Specialty was won by a beautifully presented bitch, Champion Pendleton's Jewel. Doll, as she was affectionately known, was acquired from breeder Mrs. Ann Pendleton by Dottie White.

This beautiful Maltese was the Top Toy for 1969 and 1970, winning the Quaker Oats Award for 1969. She had twenty-eight Best in Shows to

Ch. Pendleton's Jewel with her owner and handler, Dottie White. (Photo courtesy of L. Ward & F. Oberstar)

her credit and was Best of Breed and Group Second at the Westminster Dog Show in 1970.

Again, descending from Shikar Dancer was Champion Joanne-Chen's Maya Dancer, bred by Joanne Hesse and owned by Joe and Mamie Gregory. He was expertly handled throughout his career by Peggy Hogg. His impressive show career includes winning 43 Best in Shows, 134 Group Firsts, and the Toy Group at Westminster Kennel Club in 1972, making him the third Maltese to ever do so. He won the 1972 American Maltese Association National Specialty and was presented with the Quaker Oats Award for Top Group Winning Toy in 1971 and 1972.

In the early 1970s, Beverly Passe (House of Myi Maltese) acquired multiple Best in Show American Canadian Champion Salteer Glory Seeker, who was inbred on the Shikar Dancer line. An outstanding show dog and producer bred by Beverly out of Glory Seeker was Ch. Stan-Bar's Spark of Glory.

Sparky produced about thirty champions, and many of the nation's top winning Maltese carry Sparky's name in the background of their pedigrees. Only shown about five shows per year, he ranked among the top Maltese from 1976 to 1984. He received his historical final Best in Show three months shy of his 10th birthday, making him the oldest toy dog to win this award! Sparky's contribution was evident in three of his top winning relatives of the 1980s and 1990s—Champion Keoli's Small Kraft Warning, Champion Sand Island Small Kraft Lite and Champion Melodylane Sings O'Al Mar Luv.

American Canadian Bermuda Champion Oak Ridge Country Charmer caught everyone's eye in the late 1970s. Charmer was breeder-owner-handled by Carol A. Neth, completing his career with twenty-three Best in Shows, ninety Group Firsts and two American Maltese Association Specialty wins. He produced twenty-seven champions including a multiple Best in Show daughter. Carol's breeding program began in 1964, partly on Aennchen bloodlines.

The late 1970s also heralded another Dancer bred by Joanne Hesse and owned by Mrs. Blanche Tenerowicz—Champion Joanne-Chen's Mino Maya Dancer. Mino, handled by Daryl Martin (a long-time breeder of Maltese), achieved a record of 34 Best in Shows and 150 Group Firsts, setting the group record for the breed since Poona

Daryl Martin handled the top winning Ch. Joanne-Chen's Mino Maya Dancer for owner Blance Tenerowicz. (Photo by John Ashbey)

Carol Neth, guiding her Ch. Oak Ridge Country Charmer to one of his Group Firsts out of the ninety in his career.

Dancer. He was the top toy dog and the Quaker Oats winner in 1980. Mino won the American Maltese Association National Specialty in 1980 and again in 1981 from the Veteran's Class.

In 1982, Starfire, a little dog bred, owned and handled by Vicki Abbott (the author), was Winners Dog and Best of Winners at the American Maltese Association National Specialty. The grandson of Mino, his achievements included top Maltese in 1985 with eight Best in Shows and forty-five Group Firsts. Starfire was co-owned by Audrey Drake, who bred and owned the top Pekingese in 1984.

Ch. Scylla's Mina Maya Starfire with breeder-owner-handler Vicki Abbott, winning one of his forty-five Group Firsts. (Photo by Petrulius)

The number one Maltese in 1988, Ch. Louan's Apache Starfire (bred by Elsie Burke), being awarded the Group by Mr. Richard Hammond. (Photo by Carter)

The top Maltese in 1988 was a Starfire son, Champion Louan's Apache Starfire, bred and owned by Elsie Burke. Only shown for little over a year, he achieved five Best in Shows and twenty-one Group Firsts.

Down from the Villa Malta lines is a dog predominantly found in many top winners' pedigrees—Champion Non-Vel's Weejun of Carno (bred by Helen Hood). From this sire came the striking Champion Non-Vel's Weejun owned by Candace Mathes Gray and Mary Senkowski and handled by Bill Cunningham. Weejun accumulated eleven Best in Shows and more than fifty Group Firsts. He was Best of Breed at Westminster Kennel Club and Top Maltese in 1984 as well as winning the breed at the American Maltese Association National Specialty in 1985.

Champion C and M's Tootsey's Lolly Pop was the Best of Breed winner at the 1988 American Maltese Association National Specialty and again from the Veteran's class in 1992. Lolly's grandfather was Champion Non-Vels Weejun of Carno, and the C and M breeding (Mary Day and Carol Thomas) was based originally on the Villa Malta bloodlines. Lolly, owned by Sherry LeMond Ray,

Mary Day and Carole Thomas, was Best of Breed at Westminster Kennel Club twice and had six Best in Shows and about thirty Group Firsts during his career.

Ch. C and M's Tootsey's Lollypop and Mary Day, winning Best in Show under Mr. Frank Oberstar. (Photo by Fox & Cook)

IN THE PUBLIC EYE

In centuries past, the Maltese gained attention and popularity through artwork and beautiful writings primarily commissioned by aristocracy with the means to do so. The breed is fortunate in this respect because, without these things, its history would be sketchy at best. That admiration has continued to this day as you will definitely see Maltese not only in paintings and writings but also in television programs and commercials, on stage and in the movies. They also appear in newspaper and magazine advertisements, and they sometimes are even seen on greeting cards!

Several noteworthy personalities in the recent past have succumbed to the enticement of owning this breed. Liberace, the noted pianist and stage performer, and Rosemary Clooney, the popular singer, were among these proud owners. Totie Fields, the former television personality and night club comedienne, had several Maltese. Actresses Shirley Booth, Mona Freeman, Mia Farrow and Lee Remmick have owned Maltese, as has singer-actor John Davidson. Other entertainers include Tallulah Bankhead, Helen O'Connell and Gary Cooper. And who has not seen the fabulous Elizabeth Taylor with her beloved Maltese in her arms in recent years on television or in advertisements?

Serenade poses for the front of a greeting card. She is owned by Mariko Sukezaki of Japan. (Photo by Vicki Abbott)

Historically, the Maltese breed has been the pride and joy of aristocracy or a genteel society. Although this still remains the case in some instances, the breed's role in society has been somewhat expanded. Even today, however, the primary purpose of the Maltese has not changed—that of being a companion lap dog and a comforter to his master.

(Photo by Lee Guzman)

CHAPTER THREE

A Look at the Breed Standard

If a breed is recognized by the American Kennel Club, it has a breed standard, or a written description of what the ideal specimen of that particular breed should look like. This written description gives all the information a person would need to set a Maltese apart from, let's say, a Boxer. When you put together the entire list that describes a breed, you could then draw a picture, but you would have to evaluate the real dog to tell whether it has that unique quality called *type*. Type is unique to every breed; it is what, at first glance, makes you know you are looking at that particular breed. For instance, a Maltese could possess every characteristic described in the standard, yet if its character, expression and movement do not say Maltese, it does not have type and could be just another little hairy dog!

When reading the standard and attempting to compare your dog, remember that the breed standard describes the "perfect" Maltese, but no dog is perfect and no Maltese, not even the greatest dog show winner, will possess every quality asked for in its perfect form. What determines the potential for show quality is how closely the dog in question comes to the standard. In the following section, the official breed standard is presented in regular type, and commentary on the standard is in italics.

THE OFFICIAL STANDARD FOR THE MALTESE

GENERAL APPEARANCE The Maltese is a toy dog covered from head to foot with a mantle of long silky white hair. He is gentle-mannered and affectionate, eager and sprightly in action, and, despite his size, possessed of the vigor needed for the satisfactory companion.

This paragraph is what describes the Maltese type: How do you know it is a Maltese at first sight? He is the only dog in the toy group that possesses this long silky white hair! In addition, his character is described as gentle-mannered and affectionate, which should be typical for a Maltese. The breed is sweet tempered and loving. The words "eager" and "sprightly in action" are telling us about Maltese attitude—he is happy, he is a clown,

This illustration is taken from the American Maltese Association's Illustrated Guide to the Maltese Standard. *It depicts the general appearance of the Maltese at first glance.*

Type is very important. It is what distinguishes a Maltese from any other breed. (Photo by Eleanor and Dick Merget & Missy Yuhl)

and he is eager to please. And lastly, for this breed to function in its original purpose—as a companion animal—he must be sound and have the energy required for the job!

HEAD Of medium length and in proportion to the size of the dog. **The skull** is slightly rounded on top, the stop moderate. **The drop ears** are rather low set and heavily feathered with long hair that hangs close to the head. **Eyes** are set not too far apart; they are very dark and round, their black rims enhancing the gentle yet alert expression. **The muzzle** is of medium length, fine and tapered but not snipy. **The nose** is black. **The teeth** meet in an even, edge-to-edge bite or in a scissors bite.

Balance is necessary for the Maltese to have the look it needs. Balance is when all parts of the dog fit well together.

This dog's expression and silky white hair are two of the essentials for type in this breed. (Photo by Christine Pearson)

*No one part should be exaggerated to the point of disruption. Therefore, the Maltese **head** should be in proper proportion to the size of the dog—not too big for the body, nor too small. If you had a dog with a great big head and a little tiny body, that would look odd for this breed. Conversely, if the head were very tiny and the dog was overall a very big dog, that also would be unbalanced. The Maltese **skull** is slightly rounded, not apple shaped or domed. It should not resemble the exaggerated head of a Japanese Chin or a Brussels Griffon. The **ears** of a Maltese should be low set, not high like a terrier or folded or button ears like other toy breeds. They should be about*

*on a level with the outside corner of the eye on the side of the head. High-set ears prevent the feathering from hanging close to the head and create a fly-away look. The **eyes** should be a size that is in proper balance to the rest of the head—not small and beady or big and bulging. They should always be round, not almond-shaped like a Poodle, and should be dark. Maltese eyes should always have black rims—all the way around the eye. This proper combination gives the breed its gentle expression.*

*When it comes to the Maltese **bite**, two types are acceptable. One is the even, edge-to-edge bite and the other is the scissors bite, where the top teeth are slightly over the bottom teeth. Undershot, where the bottom teeth are over the top teeth, or wry mouths, where the lower jaw does not line up with the upper jaw, are not acceptable.*

NECK Sufficient length of neck is desirable as promoting a high carriage of the head.

High carriage of the head does not translate into a very long neck; in fact, length of neck should maintain overall balance. This statement refers to the regal way in which a Maltese should carry his head—not down between his shoulders or stuffed into his body. That would not be the character of a Maltese. A neck that is too long destroys balance just as a neck that is too short does. He should have just enough neck to carry his head high and proudly!

BODY Compact, the height from the withers to the ground equaling the length from the withers to the root of the tail. Shoulder blades are sloping, the elbows well knit and held close to the body. The back is level in topline, the ribs well sprung. The chest is fairly deep, the loins taut, strong, and just slightly tucked up underneath.

The Maltese appearance should be compact. In other words, a lot in a little space. Balance is achieved by the distance of the withers to the ground equaling the length of the withers to the root of the tail, which creates the illusion

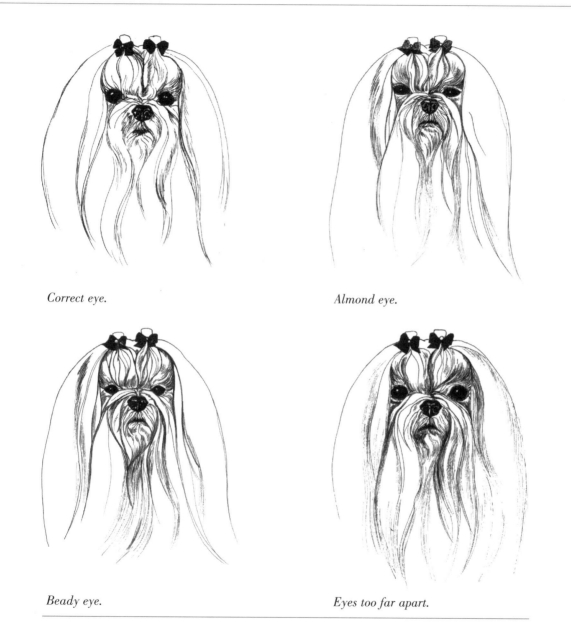

Correct eye.

Almond eye.

Beady eye.

Eyes too far apart.

These illustrations from The AMA Illustrated Guide to the Maltese Standard *show that an incorrect shape to the Maltese eye can ruin the typically sweet Maltese expression.*

its tip (the actual tailbone, not just the hair) definitely lying to the side of the quarter. If the tip does not come down so far as to lie to the side, it is an incorrect tail set, which would be called either a flag or gay tail. Other tail problems on Maltese include low tail sets and "pig" tails that curl very tightly to the extreme back of the dog, destroying the outline. The tail also should not lay flat on the back for the same reason. These types of tails can markedly change the overall appearance of the Maltese, which is so important for type.

This photo of Ch. Aennchen's Poona Dancer in wrappers gets the coat out of the way for us to view an illustration of the overall balance of the Maltese. (Photo by William E. Kelly)

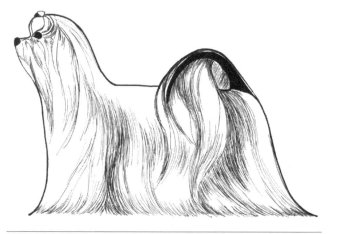

This illustration from The AMA Illustrated Guide to the Maltese Standard *shows the correct tail set for a Maltese.*

of the Maltese being much shorter in body than he truly is. The proportions should produce an off-square or slightly rectangular outline. The shoulder layback should ideally be at a 45-degree angle, and the elbows should be held close to the body. The topline should be level, both standing and in movement. It should not be dipped or roached or sloping. The ribs should be well sprung, eliminating any suggestion of a sausage or tube-like body. The chest is fairly deep, and the loins should be taut and strong with a slight tuck up (the loin being the region of the body on either side between the last rib and the hindquarter).

TAIL   A long-haired plume carried gracefully over the back, its tip lying to the side over the quarter.

The Maltese tail should be a continuation of the spine and should be carried up and over the back gracefully with

LEGS AND FEET   Legs are fine-boned and nicely feathered. Forelegs are straight, their pastern joints well knit and devoid of appreciable bend. Hind legs are strong and moderately angulated at stifles and hocks. The feet are small and round, with toe pads black. Scraggly hairs on the feet may be trimmed to give a neater appearance.

The standard stresses the importance of the legs being fine boned so as to eliminate any suggestion of coarseness.

By stressing this requirement for fine bone, the standard attempts to ensure that the Maltese will not become a dog so large and coarse that he will not be able to function in the manner for which he was bred. Feet should be small and round and may be trimmed for a neater appearance. Toe pads are required to be black, but the importance of this is an arguable point among breeders.

A lovely tail set balances the Maltese and presents a prettier picture. (Photo by Carol Andersen & Missy Yuhl)

COAT AND COLOR The coat is single, that is, without undercoat. It hangs long, flat, and silky over the sides of the body almost, if not quite, to the ground. The long hair may be tied up in a topknot or it may be left hanging. Any suggestion of kinkiness, curliness, or woolly texture is objectionable. Color, pure white. Light tan or lemon on the ears is permissible, but not desirable.

The Maltese coat is not like a Shih Tzu or a Pomeranian or a Pekingese. It is single, which means that it has no soft undercoat like some other toy breeds. (This is indeed a benefit to some because the breed does not shed like a dog with an undercoat does.) The coat should be shiny and healthy, and the density of the Maltese coat may vary. It should not stand away from the body or puff out. It should not contain any hint of kinkiness, curliness or woolly texture. In the absence of the stated objectionable characteristics, any white coat that is shiny, healthy and falls back against the body when lifted is acceptable according to the standard. The statement "almost, if not quite, to the ground" means that the coat can be almost to the ground or completely to the ground. Restated, this means "almost, if not already completely to the ground." (The word "quite" means "to the fullest extent" according to Webster.)

SIZE Weight under 7 pounds, with from 4 to 6 pounds preferred. Overall quality is to be favored over size.

Size is very important to the breed because the Maltese is a toy breed—a lap dog. A dog bred for this purpose (they were carried in the sleeves of their owners in past history) must be light and refined in his physical nature. The statement "overall quality to be favored over size" still refers to the size dictated in the standard—under 7 pounds. A Maltese should be a beautifully balanced little dog, never ungainly or clumsy in appearance. Even though his attitude may say "big dog," the Maltese is not!

GAIT The Maltese moves with a jaunty, smooth, flowing gait. Viewed from the side, he gives an impression of rapid movement, size considered. In the stride, the forelegs reach straight and free from the shoulders, with elbows close. Hind legs to move in a straight line. Cowhocks or any suggestion of hind leg toeing in or out are faults.

When moving, a Maltese should give the impression of fast, yet smooth, flowing movement. We might also mention that the word "jaunty" would indicate that he should also appear happy in attitude while that movement is going on. The forelegs should reach straight from the shoulder, and the hind legs should push out in a straight line as well. Both ends should be balanced with the proper angulation. Poor or unbalanced angulation can shorten stride and result in the dog taking shorter steps and more of them—resulting in a bouncing action rather than a smooth one. The front assembly should in no way resemble the hackney-action of a Miniature Pinscher (high flashy action in the front). A dog's hock is what is considered to be its heel, and cowhocks would mean that those heels would be turned in towards each other. Any suggestion of this or the hind legs toeing in or out would be a fault.

TEMPERAMENT For all his diminutive size, the Maltese seems to be without fear. His trust and affectionate responsiveness are very appealing. He is among the gentlest mannered of all little dogs, yet he is lively and playful as well as vigorous.

A Maltese has a fearless and dynamic temperament. He does not know he is a little dog, and his approach to life is a happy one. He is gentle mannered and will be content to lie in your lap for hours or will, in an instant, *be ready for any kind of game you can come up with for entertainment. If you do not come up with a game, he will come up with his own! A Maltese will be the most loyal of companions and will outwardly show his affection for his owner.*

IN CONCLUSION

The standard is the description of the ideal Maltese. Some things in the standard are easier to measure than others. Whether a dog has a black nose is easy to see. Weight and size are pretty easy to determine, but the aspects of balance and type require more of a trained eye to evaluate. Before attempting to evaluate a puppy or dog, you might want to contact several people with experience in the breed. Even the experts sometimes disagree with visual interpretations of the written standard. Remember that there is no perfect Maltese. Also, if you are buying your Maltese for a companion and are not considering a show dog, keep in mind that there is some reason why the breeder is not keeping this puppy to show. The standard states what is required for the ideal show specimen. Lacking a few of these qualities pertaining to conformation may eliminate a show career, but it certainly will not prevent a very lovely puppy from becoming a very important part of your family!

CHAPTER FOUR

The Choice Is Yours— Finding the Ideal Maltese

When you set out to find the Maltese of your dreams, it is best to have a plan and to know a little about what direction you are going. After all, this is an addition to your family—a lifetime investment that should involve some degree of planning and thought.

WHERE TO GO FOR HELP

Obviously, it is extremely important for the Maltese you select to have the advantage of starting life in a healthy environment. The puppy or dog should come from a responsible breeder with a reputation for producing sound stock. There are a number of good ways to start your search. The first place to contact should be the parent club of the breed. The American Maltese Association has a breeder-referral contact who can be very beneficial in helping you locate a reputable breeder in your area as well as in providing you with much needed information about Maltese. You can find their Web site address in Appendix A.

If you have a local kennel club in your area, this would be another good source for contacting breeders. The American Kennel Club, or the governing kennel club in your country, can provide you with a list of upcoming dog shows in your area. It's a really good idea to attend one or more of these shows to

Puppies that come from a responsible breeder will have been raised in very loving surroundings and will have been given a variety of new experiences. (Photo by Suzanne Johnston)

talk to Maltese breeders who might be there to exhibit their dogs.

Talk to your local veterinarian for suggestions on good breeders in the area. Beware of all the hype of advertising—a lot of very reputable long-time breeders do not even advertise their dogs because they usually have a long waiting list by word of mouth. Just because a dog or kennel is advertised does not mean it comes from a quality breeder. Be selective and understand that there are people who just use these little dogs to make a few extra dollars of income and backyard breeders who just want their pet bitch to have a litter. In these instances, the breeders may not consider the health issues when producing puppies, and the quality of the animals may be lacking. A puppy mill is a place where great quantities of dogs are mass produced to benefit the owner's pocketbook with no concern for improvement of the breed. The puppies from these circumstances can have socialization problems as well as health concerns. Take the time

to search out the best and most highly recommended situation. Even though this may require a little patience on your part if there is not a puppy available immediately, the wait will be well worth it!

The Breeder—A Contact for Life

Ideally, if you can find a breeder in your area, you will be able to visit the premises where the puppy was raised as well as view its parents and other relatives.

A good breeder is always willing to take the time to discuss with you the advantages of owning a Maltese. He will also be very helpful in pointing out any problems that exist in the breed and how they should be dealt with. You should never hesitate to ask questions during your visit about any concerns you might have.

Breeders will sometimes allow the puppies to play with their mothers long after they are weaned. Dams can teach their offspring many things including how to play and socialize with other dogs. (Photo by Linda Lamoureux)

You should also expect the breeder to ask *you* quite a number of questions. Good breeders are extremely interested in placing their puppies in loving and safe homes, and they have been known to turn away prospective buyers if they feel there might be a problem. For instance, breeders might want to know if there are young children in the family and what their ages are. They may even want to have the children come to their home to see the interaction of the children with the puppy. They may want to know if you or your children have ever owned a dog before. The breeder also will want to know where you plan to keep the new puppy—if you live in an apartment or a home and if you have a fenced-in yard. He may want to know who will be home to take care of the puppy's needs. All of these questions will help the breeder make a decision about whether you will make a good owner for the puppy.

Before You Visit, Be Informed

Not every breeder maintains a large kennel; in fact, there are very many who only keep a few quality dogs in their homes and have litters only occasionally. These people are serious hobby breeders and are likely to be on a highly

Visiting a breeder's home will give you a good idea of what experiences your puppy has had and what his relatives look like. (Photo by Judy Crowe)

recommended list from the local kennel club or parent club just as a larger kennel might be. And they may have the advantage of raising their puppies in a home environment with a lot of personal attention and socialization.

Most Maltese breeders are likely to keep their puppies until they are at least 12 to 16 weeks of age. There is a very good reason for this. By the time the litter is 8 weeks old, the puppies should be entirely weaned, or no longer nursing on their mother. During the time they are nursing, the puppies are receiving immunity from their mother. Once they stop nursing, there is a period of time when the natural immunity of the mother wears off and the puppies must develop their own immunity. They are highly susceptible to infectious diseases at this time, and it is not a good idea for the puppies to be exposed to new places.

Diseases can be transmitted on the hands and clothing of humans, so it is extremely important that the puppy you purchase have all the inoculations needed for its age. Each breeder may have a different time schedule for these shots and therefore may set a different age at which the puppies can be let go.

The best breeders breed dogs to improve

the health and quality of the breed. This is the type of person you want to deal with. A healthy Maltese puppy is happy, playful and outgoing. A puppy that appears to be listless or shy in his own environment is not a good choice. Temperament is both hereditary and environmental. A puppy that inherits good temperament can be ruined by lack of proper socialization or poor treatment. On the other hand, if the puppy comes from shy, nervous or aggressive stock and/or exhibits those characteristics, he is not a good candidate for a companion and certainly should never be used for breeding. It is extremely important that the puppy you obtain come from a breeder who has taken care to produce good Maltese temperaments and that steps have been taken early on to provide socialization.

Although Maltese puppies are small, they should feel sturdy to the touch. Their legs should be straight without any unusual bumps or malformations. Their eyes should be dark and clear with black rims and should be free from a lot of matter. The eyes should not appear red or irritated. There are several reasons that a Maltese puppy might have some red or brown stain on his face. It does not necessarily mean the puppy is unhealthy. This stain just seems to be more prevalent in some lines than others. It may or may not be a hereditary thing. It could be a problem with either the shape of the tear ducts or the pH balance of the tears themselves. If a puppy always has hair in his eyes, the eyes can be more irritated and can tear more. If a puppy is teething, the stain can sometimes be worse. The stain question has boggled the minds of experienced breeders for years (for instance, a litter can have three puppies—two with no stain and

A Maltese puppy is small but sturdy. The breeder should hold the puppy for you so you can feel his body and legs. This puppy is 14 weeks old. (Photo by Vicki Abbott)

one with!). If the puppy you are looking at has a little stain, ask your breeder about it. Some puppies outgrow this as they quit teething; some don't. (You will learn how to handle this in Chapter 8, "Grooming Your Maltese.")

A Maltese nose should be black and free of discharge. The teeth and gums should look clean and healthy, and puppy breath is always sweet! Look for any malformation of the jaw, lips or palate. A healthy puppy will have pink ears that are clean and free of any odor or discharge. Bad odor or a brownish discharge could indicate ear mites, which are extremely contagious and are an indication that this puppy has not been well cared for. Look for any danger signs of illness such as coughing or diarrhea, discharge from the nose or breaking out of the skin. A healthy Maltese puppy will have nice clean skin and a lustrous coat.

In conclusion, to avoid falling into a trap from which it will be hard to extricate yourself for years, be informed before you set out to look for your perfect companion. It is really hard after even a few days of getting attached to a puppy to have to deal with a problem that could have been avoided.

It would be an ideal world if every dog born lived a long and healthy life. Obviously, breeders can only do the their best to breed sound dogs, and they have no control over how the genes combine regardless of how careful they may be. Things can and do happen to animals just as they do to humans. There are no guarantees. That is why it is imperative for you to deal with reliable breeders. They will want to know how their dogs are doing even five, ten or fifteen years later because it makes them more educated about their own pedigrees.

First Contact with a Breeder

When you've obtained your list of names to contact, the best way to proceed is to telephone the most highly recommended breeders. If they do not have puppies available, they usually will be able to give you additional breeder recommendations in your area. Through these telephone interviews, you will be able to find out a lot about a breeder. The breeder will also want to know about you, as we mentioned before, so have your list of potential questions handy and be prepared to explain why you are looking for a Maltese. *If the conversation goes well, you will want to schedule a time for a visit.* If you have spoken to several breeders, it is a wise idea not to schedule more than one appointment per day. You will want to allow yourself the necessary time with the breeder as well as giving the breeder the courtesy of not going from one litter to another, potentially spreading infection.

When you arrive at the breeder's home, you will get some idea of how the dogs are taken care of. *Ask to see the dam of the puppy you are considering and any other relatives the breeder may have on the premises.* Often, the sire will not be available because he may belong to another breeder who lives somewhere else, possibly far away. *Ask if there are pictures available for you to look at to see what the dogs looked like when they had long hair.* Most breeders will clip the hair on the dogs not being shown, leaving them in a comfortable "puppy trim." This is also safer for the puppies as they are nursing.

By looking at the dam or other relatives, you will get an idea of temperament, size and coat that adults in this breeder's line possess. *Ask if your puppy will be smaller or larger than his relatives based on what the breeder knows to be the growth pattern of his dogs.* This, believe it or not, can be the biggest bone of contention between a buyer and the breeder from which the puppy was purchased. Run from a breeder who promises you that a dog will be an exact size. Even if they know their dogs' growth rate and have been breeding for many years, they still can only estimate. If the breeder you bought your dog from tells you that the dog will not get to be over 3 pounds, and he turns out to be a whopping 13, something is wrong.

Beware of breeders who advertise "teacup Maltese." There is no such thing, and it is used as a gimmick to attract people who prefer a tiny dog. The Maltese standard states that the breed is to be under 7 pounds, with 4 to 6 pounds preferred. A reputable breeder will not breed for tinier and tinier Maltese because that would not be improving the breed by attempting to breed as close to the standard as possible. However, there are many small but sturdy Maltese under the 4-pound suggestion. Sometimes a good breeder will end up with a smaller dog in a litter because the genes somewhere in the background combined to produce small. Many of the earlier Maltese champions in this century in the United States were 3-pound dogs. The breeder may then decide to part with the puppy to a good pet home rather than use it as part of their breeding program. If your preference is tiny, still go only to reliable breeders and ask if they ever get any smaller puppies in their litters.

Ask the breeder if you can take the puppy away from his littermates to a different part of the house so you can look at him a little closer and see how he interacts with you. The smells should remain the same, so the puppy should still feel secure. This is a good place to determine temperament in a puppy. Maltese should be friendly and bouncy! This will also give you the opportunity to inspect the puppy more closely. Remember what you learned to look for in a healthy puppy and ask questions about anything that concerns you.

Lastly, make sure you *ask the breeder what the health issues are for the breed and whether there are any*

A basketful of love, but only for just the right the owner! (Photo by Julie Phillips)

potential problems you should watch out for. The breeder from whom you purchase your puppy, among other things, should be breeding to improve the health of the breed. Although breeders are obviously not expected to have a veterinary degree, they should have some knowledge of what problems exist and what to look for as the dog gets older.

DECISION DAY

When you have decided to take that final step and purchase your puppy, the breeder should provide you with five things: a contract, a bill of sale or registration papers, a diet sheet, a health record and a pedigree. Do not leave with your new puppy without them!

The **contract** outlines the breeder's guarantees and the responsibilities of the buyer. On the contract should appear the puppy's breed and registered name (if he has one), his AKC registration number or litter number if he is not yet registered and the names and numbers of his sire and dam. It should also include the breeder's name, address and telephone number. Your name as the buyer should be listed along with your address and telephone number and the date you purchased the puppy. The contract should state the price of the puppy and should contain a health guarantee that your purchase of this puppy is contingent upon his passing a veterinarian's examination. It may also state how long you have to do this, which ideally would be within twenty-four to forty-eight hours from the time you take your puppy home. This time limit may vary with breeders. The contract should state whether there are any special arrangements between the two parties. Many times breeders will require that the puppy be spayed or neutered before they will give registration papers to the new owner. This is their guarantee that the puppy will not be bred. Since some puppies are too young to have surgery at the time of purchase, the owner may send verification of the surgery from

a veterinarian to the breeder at a later date. The breeder will then send the registration papers to the owner. This is why, if you do not receive the registration papers at the time of purchase, you will need a bill of sale. The bill of sale can be a part of the contract. Finally, you should both sign the contract. Read the contract carefully and ask for any explanations if needed.

The **registration certificate** is issued by a country's governing kennel club. It records the transfer of ownership from the breeder to you as the new owner. It should always be filled out and signed by the breeder. When you sign your name and send it in, your puppy is permanently recorded in the files at the kennel club. What you choose to name your puppy on the registration papers cannot be changed in the future, so be real sure before you make the final decision!

A **diet sheet** is a must if your puppy is going to make a smooth transition from his current home to your home. Changing a puppy's diet drastically in a short period of time can cause severe problems to his little digestive system, especially on a young puppy that has only been weaned for a few weeks. Part of the reason you are buying a happy, healthy puppy is because the breeder has taken the care to make sure the puppy has had the best nutrition possible. The diet sheet should include details of what kind and amount of food the puppy has been receiving. It should state the number of times a day the puppy should be fed and whether there has been any vitamin supplementation. It should also give a recommendation for the next few months or even up to a year of age, at which time you may need to change to adult food. Most breeders have a definite opinion about what foods are good for their breed. Follow their instructions explicitly—their ideas are usually based on vast experience with their particular breed. Many dog foods on the market today will cause problems in the Maltese breed with either the digestive system or the skin and coat. Listen to your breeder and stick to the program!

The **health record** will list for you the inoculations your puppy has had as of the time of purchase. Most puppies have had all the shots they need as a young dog by the time they are 16 weeks of age. These inoculations protect the puppies against hepatitis and potentially fatal diseases such as distemper and canine parvovirus. A booster for these inoculations will follow at a prescribed time—ask the breeder what he recommends. Inoculation procedures are changing as more research is done. It is extremely important for you to know what procedures have been followed for your puppy so that the veterinarian you choose can continue with the appropriate care.

Every purebred dog has a **pedigree**. Your puppy's pedigree is his "family tree." It is a document that will authenticate his ancestors back to at least the third generation. It *does not* mean your puppy is a show-quality dog. Unethical puppy dealers may try to convince you that, just because a dog has a pedigree, it automatically makes the dog more expensive or of championship quality. This is far from the case—the puppy's entire

Male or female? Bigger or smaller? Personality? Pedigree? There are a lot of things to consider, so be as informed as possible before making a decision. (Photo by Julie Phillips)

pedigree may be one of registered pets. A dog only has to be purebred to be registered. On the other hand, if your puppy's pedigree contains many champions—especially within the first three generations—you can expect that the breeder you are buying from has actively been producing and exhibiting quality dogs. This still does not mean your puppy is show quality; however, it does indicate the overall quality of the breeding program.

SHIPPING AS AN ALTERNATIVE

If you cannot find a good breeder close to you or if you are looking for a dog from a particular breeder, it may be necessary to have the puppy shipped to you on approval. The usual procedure is to find a nonstop flight from the breeder's airport to yours on a priority counter-to-counter basis. Before you have the puppy shipped, the breeder should send you photos or videos and a pedigree to help in the decision. When having a puppy shipped, always depend on the breeder's advice for how to ship the dog and when. He will know the best possible way to transport the puppy with the least amount of stress. He will probably also want to know a great deal about you before he will ship you the puppy because he has not been able to meet and visit with you. Many breeders require references before they will ship one of their puppies.

If you do have a puppy shipped to you, you will probably have a certain amount of time to decide, or "approve," the puppy. Most breeders will want you to do this within a very short time period. Talk to your breeder, fully understand his expectations and have something to that effect in writing before you have the puppy shipped.

THE POSSIBILITY OF AN ADULT DOG

Many times, breeders will keep a puppy until it is a little older because he looks very promising as a show dog. Then, for whatever reason—possibly the dog grows a little too large or stays a little too small, or maybe the permanent teeth do not come in correctly—the decision is made to find a good home for the dog. In this case, the dog has been groomed and cared for as a possible show prospect, and the coat and condition as well as the training on the dog are probably superb. This type of

situation would be quite a find for someone looking for a slightly older dog. Maltese are perpetual puppies. They never know they grew up!

You actually will not find much difference in attitude between a 16-week-old puppy and a $1^1/_2$-year-old dog. Older Maltese readily adapt to new places and delight in the personal attention they get—after all, at the breeder's house they are one of many; at your house, guess who gets all the attention! In other instances, breeders may have a male or female they no longer wish to use for breeding but would love for the dog to be neutered or spayed and live out his life in a private home as a pampered pet. After all, that *is* what they were bred for.

Though most breeders would hate to admit it, a Maltese will love anyone. An adult Maltese will readily adapt to a new situation when given loving care. With an adult, you can skip the problems that raising a puppy involves. Elderly people often prefer adult dogs because they are easier to manage and adapt more readily to household rules. An adult is a very good choice depending on your circumstances. There are some things to consider, however, before you make the decision. If an adult dog has never been around very vocal, active children, it may be intimidated. Or if you have another dog at your home that the Maltese has not been exposed to, he may or may not get along with the other dog. If the other dog is bigger, it may even be dangerous for the Maltese. A Maltese is very playful and does not realize his small size. He may incite a larger friend into romping and playing in a manner that will result in an unintentional accident. Adult dogs may or may not fit into your

What's for dinner? Willy was 10 months old when he went to live with Rosemarie and Ray Saccardi, and as you can see, he's a part of the family! (Photo by Rosemarie & Ray Saccardi)

routine. Talk to the breeder to find out the habits of the young adult or older dog. One thing is for sure—when you decide on a little older Maltese, it provides greater certainty with respect to quality because the dog is mature. What you see is certainly what you get with no surprises later!

SELECTING A SHOW-QUALITY PUPPY

If you are looking for a puppy as a show prospect, you must find a breeder who has developed a reputation for breeding and exhibiting winning Maltese over an extended period of time. You will have to depend on this breeder to help you

evaluate potential show puppies based on the years of experience he has had in selecting dogs for the show ring. Do not fall for unscrupulous breeders who advertise show-quality puppies at 8 weeks of age. Unless this person is a certified foreseer of the future, he cannot tell you what is going to happen between now and the time the dog is old enough to show! Most responsible breeders can label their puppies as having "show potential" at 12 to 16 weeks of age. But even then, you are taking a risk one way or another if you invest a great amount of money in a show dog at this age. We strongly suggest that, if you are serious about showing your Maltese, you should wait until a puppy is 6 to 12 months of age before making any decisions.

It is obvious that the older the puppy is, the easier it is to determine how it will turn out. So many things can change on a Maltese between 12 weeks and 1 year of age. Permanent teeth come in at 6 months old, and until that time, the bite can change one way or another. A proper-size "show potential" Maltese at 6 months old can either stop growing and end up too small or hit a growth spurt and end up too big. Coat texture can change over a period of months in a good or bad way. Many of the flaws that would keep a dog out of the show ring are barely noticeable to the average person and do not inhibit the Maltese from being a wonderful companion. However, they may keep the puppy from ever being a winner. Since the purchase of a show dog is a greater investment than the purchase of a pet, the prospective buyer must depend on the advice of a good breeder. Attending dog shows to see the quality of Maltese in the show ring is a good educational experience before purchasing a show puppy. There are also a number of good books on the breed that can be very helpful in learning more about the breed and what to look for in a show prospect. The more informed you are, the better you will be able to make a good decision about your potential show dog.

Remember that your show puppy should meet the requirements for not only the look required in

A puppy with show potential is best chosen at an older age, when there is less likelihood that anything could go wrong to keep him out of the ring. (Photo by Pamela McDonald)

the standard but also the temperament. A show puppy will need to be tremendously outgoing and capable of handling new situations—his show career will demand this.

THE RESCUE MALTESE

Unfortunately, sometimes this beautiful breed is faced with situations that are the nightmares every breeder has about placing a puppy. For an endless list of reasons and through no fault of their own, some Maltese end up needing to be rescued. Rescue dogs come in all ages and sizes. Many are very sweet and just need a home. There are rescue organizations in almost all parts of the country, and some are dedicated to the rescue of just this breed. The American Maltese Association Rescue is one of the organizations dedicated to the rescue and placement of needy Maltese. There is usually a minimal adoption fee that goes toward helping to run the organization or to paying for veterinarian bills for the dogs themselves. Almost all rescue organizations require that the dog be spayed or neutered. Many volunteers spend many hours rescuing these little Maltese and preparing them for their new adoptive homes. They are very careful in their selection of new owners for these special dogs. If you are interested in adopting one of these little ones and can provide the loving home they need, contact one of the rescue organizations to fill out an application.

(Photo by Noreen Bieniek)

C H A P T E R   F I V E

Living with Your Maltese

Before you bring your new puppy into your home, you must make preparations and have a plan. Your life will never be the same once you have owned a Maltese—we hear this over and over. Once a Maltese owner, always a Maltese owner. You can make the first few weeks with your new puppy the best possible by knowing and being prepared for his physical needs as well as understanding the temperament of the breed as it relates to training.

THE FIRST INTRODUCTIONS

Believe me, everyone who enters your home after you get your Maltese puppy will know the Maltese is there. Maltese are one of the friendliest breeds that exist and anyone's lap is a fair target! Introduce everyone who enters your household to your puppy; it is good for him to get to know other people and to increase his socialization skills. However, the Maltese is not a particularly good breed for very small children. Toddlers are usually not able to understand that a very little Maltese must be handled with care. Care must be taken when small children are around to keep them supervised.

Do not let a small child take off holding the dog in his arms. If a puppy is dropped or squeezed hard, it can cause much damage. On the other hand, a slightly older child can be taught to care for a puppy's needs and will make a great companion for a Maltese. Two of our Maltese are lucky to own two such wonderful young girls who reside in Florida. They each have their own dog, and I'm not sure who runs out of energy first, the Maltese or the girls! But a Maltese will love to be held, won't mind having a

Vicki's daughter Tara found her love for the breed at a very young age. Closely supervised, a younger child can learn to handle a Maltese puppy carefully. (Photo by Vicki Abbott)

Two sisters—each with her own special dog. Jessica and Jenna Blick always find time to relax with their Maltese buddies.

pretty hat put on its head or being dressed in a sweater and will definitely find spending the evening on the couch to watch television a treat!

Your puppy should go places with you—to the post office, the market, the mall or wherever it is safe to take him. You will create a stir wherever you choose to go because this breed tends to be a crowd pleaser. A Maltese is a happy dog and will take most situations in stride, but introducing him gradually to different everyday events will develop his personality to the fullest. Traffic, strange noises, hyperactive children and strange animals can be very intimidating to a small puppy when he has not been anywhere new before. Speak to him gently, letting him know that you are there, and make every new experience an enjoyable one.

Maltese are compatible with other dogs as long as they are supervised until you feel their safety is not an issue. Some dogs feel threatened when a new puppy is brought into the home, so if you already have a dog and are adding to your family, take care that the older dog gets a lot of attention as well. Try to be present at all times when the two are together at first to step in if there are any problems. Do not force the issue; in time, you can gradually get the desired results.

A very small puppy should be watched when running around; he could get stepped on or have a door closed on him—it has happened. He can also pick up small objects in his mouth and swallow or choke on them quickly, so you will need to puppy-proof your house for his safety. I recently was told of a Maltese that decided to steal her owner's sewing that was left on the bed for only a second. After surgery on the dog's stomach to remove the needle, she was fine. But had the owner not noticed the sewing missing and had she not taken her to the vet immediately, this could have been a tragedy. Anything you have heard about how to make a home safe for a toddler applies to a puppy as well.

Housecleaning products and anything that is poisonous, such as antifreeze, should be put somewhere that the puppy (or dog, as he grows) cannot reach even by jumping. Plants can also be poisonous. Diffenbachia or dumbcane are examples of plants to put out of reach. At Christmas time, remember to put Poinsettias in a safe place.

There are plenty of toys, ropes and other things made for a dog to chew on that can be purchased for your puppy at the pet store. It is always a lot of fun to walk up and down the aisle to pick out new toys. Some items sold for dogs to chew on will get gummy or break off, which could cause internal damage. Rawhide chew bones tend to do this and can be hazardous to your puppy.

If you care about retaining the coat around the dog's mouth for show or just for the sake of appearance, forget anything that will tear the hair, anything that has dye in it that will rub off and anything that gets sticky while being chewed. Amazingly enough, we have even heard stories of small latex toys being swallowed whole, so it is a good idea to be watchful. It must be said that,

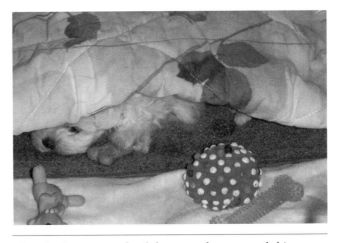

Puppies love toys and safe bones to chew on, and this clown is definitely making sure his property is protected! (Photo by Julie Phillips)

although Maltese generally are not destructive or habitual chewers, puppies do go through a time when they lose their baby teeth and the permanent ones come in. During this time, they will be more prone to chew on things, so plan ahead and avoid disasters.

KNOWING THE MALTESE TEMPERAMENT FOR TRAINING

Know one thing for sure—a Maltese or any small dog will not respond well to physical reprimands of any kind. In fact, it may well injure the dog for life, so put away your rolled-up newspapers, fly swatters or whatever you think may be a good training tool. Depend on the inflection in your voice and the sweet Maltese temperament that only wants to please! Your new puppy is in a new place with new smells and new people. He will be quite confused for a while and may not be immediately ready for training until he settles in a little bit. That does not mean you cannot start being consistent about what you expect from him—it *does* mean you must be very patient. Stay aware of the sensitivity level of your Maltese. Maltese respond well to lots of praise but do not respond to yelling or being struck. Never get so irritated as to shake your Maltese puppy because you could cause irreparable damage. A stern "no" is all that is required on a consistent basis to correct any kind of unwanted behavior. Maltese are very smart.

There are many Maltese all over the country that have achieved advanced obedience titles and have won many awards. Do not feel that because a

Maltese is small, he cannot perform. He will surprise you with his big heart for whatever you want him to do.

Learning "No"

It may be that the most important command your puppy will ever learn is the word "no." This command should probably start on the first day home. Be consistent and wisely choose the things you don't wish your puppy to do. It is confusing to the puppy if you allow him to do some things on one day and not on the next. Everyone in the family needs to be familiar with the set of planned rules for this new member of the family. Be consistent and you will see results amazingly fast. The "no" command should probably be reserved for situations in which the puppy might harm himself or to keep him from harming something or someone else. Chewing on furniture, for example, is not acceptable. Relieving himself in the wrong place is not acceptable. Dashing across the street in the path of a car is not acceptable—you get the idea. The trick to this is that you must really catch the puppy in the act of doing something for this to be effective. Telling your puppy "no" an hour after you find the furniture chewed is only going to get you a strange and confused look.

HOUSETRAINING YOUR HOUSE DOG

Maltese are really not hard to housetrain whether they are small puppies or adults. More often than not, the problems more have to do with the training methods and the trainer than with the dog's inability to learn.

The major difference between housetraining a puppy versus an older dog is that the younger puppy tends to forget with greater speed and will probably need to be reminded more often. Train your puppy; don't let him train you. Puppies will quickly learn what they can put over on you and what they can't. If they are allowed into the house or a room because they are barking or whining, they will develop this habit for life and presto!—You're trained! You must become the leader for your new little dog to follow. If you do not, guess who will?

You must provide the rules by which the puppy abides. If there are no rules, the puppy will make his own, and you will end up with a real little nuisance that no one will want to be around. Remember, the key to successfully training your dog is in the relationship established between the two of you at the outset.

It is much easier for your puppy to learn a good habit than it is for him to unlearn a bad one. The trick to successful housetraining is to avoid bad habits before they begin.

We recommend that you crate-train your Maltese in order to housetrain him. A crate is the little fiberglass kennel (size 100 for small dogs) that is usually used for transporting small animals. Breeders will use these crates for many purposes. We use them to travel with the dog in the car safely and to carry a dog around at dog shows. If we set them around the dog room, the dogs love to run in and out of them while playing, and they will sleep in them at night. A Maltese loves having a little den to retreat to for rest and privacy. It is not cruel to keep your puppy in a crate such as this to keep him from wandering around and soiling your carpet wherever he pleases. Use of a crate reduces housetraining time and avoids the stress caused by constantly having to correct the puppy for relieving himself in the wrong place. These crates are available at pet stores and should be on your list of priority items to buy before your new puppy comes home with you. The crate used for housetraining should only be large enough for the puppy to stand up and stretch out in comfortably.

Begin by using the crate as the place to feed your puppy. Keep the door closed and latched while the puppy is eating. When he has finished his meal, immediately open the crate and carry the puppy to where you would like him to learn to eliminate. Some Maltese owners want their puppy to be trained to the outside. You can accomplish this even if you do not have a backyard if you take your puppy outside on a leash. However, if you would prefer to train your puppy to the indoors first or as an alternate solution on a rainy day, you can put down papers in a corner (the same place every time) or use hospital pads that are absorbent and disposable. These pads can be bought at a pet store or a medical-supply store. They work great, especially on a trip.

If you consistently take your puppy to the same spot, you will reinforce the habit of going there for that purpose. The key word here is *consistently*. You, as the leader, must be the one who is consistent with taking the puppy out at the same times every day and not allowing him to make mistakes. Most dogs, whatever age they are, will eliminate after eating and drinking. They will also be ready to relieve themselves when they first wake up and after playing. Obviously, a young puppy will probably need to go out more times during the day than he will as he gets older and is able to control himself better. Watch for your puppy to sniff the floor before he needs to go out and take him out before an accident happens. Maltese are also notorious for going in circles when looking for a place to go. When you are not watching your puppy, he should be in his crate with the door latched securely. Do not give in to his complaints about being away from you and in the crate. He needs to learn to stay there and to do so without unnecessary complaining. If he creates too much racket, tap on the top of the crate and give the "no" command. This will usually get the puppy to understand that this kind of behavior will not result in freedom.

You can housetrain your puppy to the inside on papers or pads, to the outside in the grass or to an exercise pen on the patio or in the yard. (Photo by Judy Crowe)

At night, you can take your puppy out right before bedtime and then put him in his crate for the night. If you want him with you, put him right beside the bed where you can tap on the crate and tell him "no" if he creates a disturbance. Your puppy may be lonely the first few nights he is away from his dam and littermates, but your reassuring voice telling him to go to sleep should be enough.

The priority in the morning is to let your puppy out. Do not wait for him to make a mistake in the crate or let him vocalize his need to go out for any length of time. If you are not at home a majority of the day, you obviously cannot leave your puppy in the crate. Find a small area in your home that you can partition off with a child gate or a puppy fence. Make the area large enough that the puppy will not have to relieve himself next to his bed or his food and water. This would preferably be an area that is not carpeted.

Because your puppy will not be able to go all day without being let out, place some newspaper or a few hospital pads in the spot where you want your puppy to eliminate. When you are at home, you will need to take the puppy to this same place at the appropriate time so he knows that this one particular spot is where you expect him to eliminate. He can then sleep in his crate at night.

GOING FOR A WALK

A Maltese does not need a big heavy collar and lots of tags attached. This is too heavy on his little neck. Start off with a very lightweight soft collar. After a few attempts at scratching it off, he will get used to it being there. Leave it on for a short period of time and then remove it. Gradually increase the amount of time you leave the collar on until he doesn't notice it any more. Once you have accomplished this, you can attach a lightweight leash to the collar. Allow the puppy to walk around while you hold the leash loosely so he does not feel guided at first. Soon he will get used to something being attached to the collar and will want to go with you.

It is really not a necessity for your Maltese to wear a collar all the time if he is kept indoors (which he should be). Collars can tend to catch in the long hair and end up twisted or too tight around the neck. If you go outside with your dog, however, always put on his collar and leash unless you are in a fenced backyard. Having your dog on the end of a leash is protection for both you and him. You never know what you may encounter along your walk. If you are having problems

Leash-training your Maltese is important for a variety of reasons. Here, the Maltese are being exercised safely while traveling. (Photo by Vicki Abbott)

getting your puppy to walk along with you, try holding a treat in your hand and coaxing him gently to come a little bit at a time. Praise him enthusiastically and continue to do so as you move along. Above all, make these lessons fun for the puppy. He should look forward to walks with you. Remember that a little dog has to take a lot more steps than you do to get somewhere. Stay tuned in to whether he is getting tired and needs to head home. A Maltese is not an appropriate companion for a 5-mile jogger!

A LIFE-SAVING COMMAND

Learning to come on command may save your dog's life. Your dog must have the understanding that this command must be obeyed without question. Make the learning experience for this command pleasant and associate it with lots of praise and affection. Treats are good to give for a job well done. To use this command effectively, your puppy must learn his name. Constant repetition will be the best way to accomplish this. Use his name every time you talk to your puppy. Never give the "come" command unless you are in a situation in which you are sure the dog will come to you. Bad habits are hard to break. A young puppy will usually come to you because he is entirely dependent upon you. As the dog gets older, he may get more independent, causing his attention to be drawn more to his surroundings. With this in mind, it is a good idea to start this training early.

Start your puppy's training when he is already moving towards you. This is the perfect time to give the command to "come," and you should

praise him highly when he gets to you. Never start training for this with the dog running around loose and expect him to automatically stop what he is doing just because you want him to—it won't happen on a consistent enough basis for him to learn the command. The next step would be to put on his collar and leash to make sure he will come to you when you call him. It is never a good idea to chase or punish your puppy. By doing this in the early stages of his learning the command, he will associate the learning with fear. The response you want should be a positive one. A puppy or dog should feel that coming to his owner is going to result in something very nice for him!

SIT OR STAY

It can be a lot of fun to train your puppy if you remember that his attention span is that of a youngster and that he is not going to put up with much for very long periods of time. Your training periods should be kept short and productive. Sometimes it is nice for your dog to know how to "sit" if you'd like him to wait while you are serving his food instead of jumping all over you. It is also nice for him to know this command if you have guests over and do not want him to be a pest.

To start teaching this command, first put a collar and a lead on your puppy. With your puppy standing beside you, give the command to "sit" and then reach down and exert gentle pressure on his rear. When he is in the correct position, praise him highly even though it was really you who got him there! A food treat can also be very enjoyable and can make the experience a pleasant one for the

Ch. Louan's Cherokee Frost illustrates the sitting position nicely and has won awards for his performance. (Photo by Elsie Burke)

puppy. If the puppy makes an attempt to get up, correct him and return him to the sitting position. He needs to learn that you will be the one who decides the appropriate time to get up.

Remember that your puppy's attention span will not be very long, so start off with just a few seconds and increase the time a little with each succeeding training session. When you decide it is time for the puppy to get up, call his name and say "OK." Then make as big a fuss as you can over him with lots of praise and, of course, a treat!

The "stay" command should only be attempted once the puppy has learned to sit. Put on the puppy's collar and leash and give him the command to "sit" facing you. Then take a few steps back. If the puppy attempts to get up to come to you, raise your hand with your palm toward the dog and firmly give the command "sit, stay!" You may need to go to the puppy to put him back in place if he does not correct this himself, but in any case, he must be corrected immediately for the lesson to be effective. Once your puppy begins to understand what it is you want him to do, you may be able to take more and more steps back. It is important for him to understand that the command must be obeyed no matter how far away you are. As with the "sit" command, it is you who will decide how long the puppy must "stay." At that point, do not call the puppy to you. Walk back to him and say "OK," letting him know that the command is over. When you feel comfortable that your Maltese puppy will obey this command, you can start calling him to you. With advanced training, it is even possible that you might be able to walk out of the room or entirely out of sight and still expect your Maltese to obey the command.

DOWN, PLEASE

When you are pleased that your puppy has learned the "sit" and "stay" commands, you can progress to teaching the "down" command. It is very confusing for a really young puppy to learn a lot of these things at once, so it may be a while before you actually get to this. The "down" command is good if you want your dog to remain in one place for a very long time because the position is more comfortable for the dog. This command may be a little more difficult to teach and may require more patience on your part to keep the training sessions positive.

Place your Maltese, with his leash and collar on, in front of you in a sitting position. With a treat in your right hand and the leash in your left, put the treat under the dog's nose and slowly bring your hand down to the ground. As your dog follows the treat to the ground with his head and neck, exert light pressure on his shoulders and say, "down." Don't battle with the dog and continue pushing real hard if he resists. If this happens, reach down and slide the dog's front feet toward you until he is lying down. As the dog's forelegs slide, continue to move the treat forward and repeat

"Down" all the way nicely and watching for the okay to get up! (Photo by Julie Phillips)

"down" until he is in the right position. He should be all the way on the ground with his forelegs out in front of him.

HEELING FOR YOUR SAFETY

I am amazed by the number of accidents I have heard about in which owners or their dogs have been injured because of the little dog dashing between or around their feet. A Maltese will do this—they just want to be everywhere you are and to get there before you do! Because they are so small, they can be greatly injured and so can you. Teaching your dog to "heel" can eliminate this problem and can make life more pleasant for both of you. When your Maltese learns this command, he will walk on your left side with his shoulder next to your leg no matter which direction you are going.

Change your dog's collar from the one he regularly wears to a lightweight, rounded leather collar to begin this training. This will indicate to the dog that there is something different about this training and that this is not just you and he going out for a casual walk. Chain collars can get tangled in Maltese hair, and this is why we recommend the rounded leather. Start out with your Maltese on your left side. Your leash should cross your body from the dog's collar to your right hand. Fold the excess part of the leash into your right hand and keep your left hand on the leash to make corrections to the dog. A quick, gentle jerk on the leash with your left hand as you are walking will keep your dog from lunging side to side. You can also keep him from darting ahead or between your legs. Whenever you correct your dog, give him the "heel" command. If he maintains the proper position at your side, leave the leash loose. Give him lots of praise when he performs correctly. (A scratch or two behind the ears wouldn't hurt, either!)

SMALL BUT SMART

If you are patient and keep the training sessions a happy time for your Maltese, there will be no limit to what he can accomplish. A Maltese, remember, was bred to be a companion and to please. They will go to extremes to do what you would like them to do if they understand what you want and you are consistent. They may be small, but there are a lot of brains and heart in that small body! The effort you expend now to train your dog will be rewarded with many years of fun times with your companion.

Gucci, one of Julie Phillips' obedience dogs, shows that beauty and brains are both very much Maltese traits! (Photo by Julie Phillips)

(Photo by Vicki Abbott)

CHAPTER SIX

Keeping Your Maltese Happy and Healthy

The most important two people to your puppy (besides you), now and in the future, are his breeder and the veterinarian you choose. If purchased from a responsible breeder, your puppy has been provided with quality care from the time he was born until you brought him home. It is now up to you to take care of your Maltese and to make wise decisions when it comes to his health and well-being.

CHOOSING THE RIGHT VETERINARIAN

It is extremely important that you choose a veterinarian who has had the experience of working with very small dogs and, in particular, Maltese. Be aware that not all veterinarians give the same quality of service. Some veterinarians in rural areas are only used to working with horses, cows and larger animals. The care and the recommendations made can be vastly different for the small breed. Spending a little extra time finding the right veterinarian can save you the extra cost involved with improper diagnosis or treatment. We suggest that you ask your breeder for a recommendation for a good veterinarian to take your puppy to. If you are far away from your breeder, it might be a good idea to contact friends who have small dogs to see what their experiences and recommendations are.

Obtain a reference for a veterinarian who is known to be knowledgeable about toy dogs' needs. Dr. Janice Price not only is a veterinarian, she is also a Maltese breeder, which obviously makes her a very wise choice! (Photo by Janice W. Price, DVM)

Visit this veterinarian with your puppy within the first twenty-four to forty-eight hours that he is in your possession. Call ahead to make an appointment. Do not get any vaccinations or have any work done; just have the veterinarian look over your puppy to give him an overall clearance on his health. This will give you some idea of the bedside manner of your veterinarian. He or she should have very gentle hands on your toy dog and should not recommend many things that are not necessary for the puppy to have. Always check with your breeder before having any additional treatments given to your very young puppy. If you are satisfied with this veterinarian, you will probably only need to return for annual checkups, in the case of an emergency, for booster vaccinations later on and for spaying or neutering when necessary.

THE FIRST CHECKUP

When you take your puppy in for his first checkup, make sure you take him in his crate. This will give him more of a feeling of security and will keep him away from the other dogs that might be in the office. Remember, germs are transmitted through contact with other dogs, and your puppy is still very young. If a dog is at the veterinarian, it is either sick or there for a routine checkup—don't take a chance. When you are called in to see the doctor, take your puppy gently out of the crate and introduce him to the situation, talking to him all the while. You will have a much brighter future for routine visits if you make this one as pleasant as possible! Have the veterinarian check your puppy's eyes. They should be free of discharge, dark and clear. He should check the nose and throat for any signs of infection. The mouth should be checked for healthy teeth and gums. Ears should be inspected for signs of infection or ear mites. The veterinarian will probably need to check your puppy's stool for any sign of worms or other problems. (You can collect a sample and take it with you to the first visit to save time.) He will look at your puppy's legs and back for any abnormalities, will listen to his heart and respiration and will feel his abdomen. Lastly, he will check the skin condition and coat.

Most pets have some kind of minor flaw that will not affect their health or ever cause any kind of real problem. But if the veterinarian finds any kind of serious problem, you will want to consider the consequences of keeping the puppy and what is involved for the rest of his life. Sometimes a breeder's veterinarian will not catch a problem early in the puppy's life that crops up a few weeks later, so even the breeder may not be aware of a problem. If this should occur, contact your breeder immediately. A reputable breeder will want to know about any problem and will stand behind his guarantee of a healthy puppy.

Remember to make a list of questions you would like to ask your new veterinarian before you go. He will probably ask you questions about your puppy's eating and elimination habits and whether you have noticed any problems.

Do not skip this first visit within a few days of acquiring your puppy. A dog can appear perfectly healthy but have a problem that is not apparent to the average layman. Veterinary medicine has come a long way, even in the last few years. Many times there are specialists, just as there are for humans, who deal with specific problems in our pets to help them live longer and healthier lives. Starting out with the best care can put your mind at rest that your puppy is happy and healthy, and it can give you the right person to call for any future problem.

Your Maltese should be checked for any signs of eye, nose or throat infection. (Photo by Janice W. Price, DVM)

IMMUNIZATIONS

When an animal is immune to something, it has antibodies in its system that will attack and destroy germs before they cause a disease or an illness. When the animal is not immune and is exposed to something to which it is susceptible, it will get sick and therefore automatically start making antibodies to fight the particular disease. That is basically what a vaccine does artificially in a healthy dog's system. The disease, which has been altered so it cannot produce the actual disease, is injected into the dog's body, forcing it to develop antibodies to that particular disease. If ever exposed, the dog would then have the antibodies to fight off the disease. These antibodies are very specific to one type of disease.

When your puppy receives a vaccination, his body is working overtime to try to develop immunity to that disease. A puppy or dog that is compromised or stressed in any way should never receive a vaccine. If your dog is sick, he will not be able to develop the appropriate immunities needed. Some drugs depress or prevent antibodies from forming, so if your pet is receiving medication, you should check with the doctor before the dog is given an inoculation. Before you bring your puppy home, the breeder will have given your puppy what is called a *puppy series*. The inoculation given during a puppy series usually contains the distemper and parvovirus vaccines and may contain others such as hepatitis or parainfluenza. Maltese breeders usually exclude the Leptospirosis vaccine because this disease has been virtually eliminated, and Maltese and toy dogs in general seem to have severe anaphylactic reactions to it. The puppy series is given in two to three doses, four weeks apart.

The dam's immunity is present in the puppies up until a certain age. No one knows for sure when this wears off, probably between 6 and 12 weeks of age. At least one vaccine should be administered after this time, at about 16 weeks of age, just to make sure the maternal antibodies have not interfered with the puppy developing his own immunity. Your puppy's next vaccination in this series after 16 weeks of age should not be until he is 1 year old. Again, follow your breeder's advice pertaining to your particular puppy's vaccination schedule.

The challenge in the veterinary community has been to produce safer and more effective vaccinations for our animals. Recently, there has been quite a bit of research and numerous articles written about the protocol used in immunizing our pets on a yearly basis. Many veterinarians feel there

is no justification today for annual revaccination, and they are recommending an every-three-year schedule instead. Talk to your breeder and to your veterinarian about this. Some states require that rabies vaccinations be given every three years, and some are yearly. Find out what is required in your area. A puppy should not receive the rabies vaccine until he is at least 6 months of age because it is one of the hardest vaccines on a Maltese or a toy dog's system.

Many veterinarians also recommend that your dog not be given a vaccine with a variety of things in it. They recommend monovalent or bivalent vaccines, which means that in one shot there will only be one, or at most two, diseases for the dog to have to develop an immunity to at one time.

Many well-meaning pet owners do not realize that the immunizations and other treatments they allow to be administered to their animals could very well be part of the problems the animals are experiencing later on in life. Repeated inoculation of our dogs with killed or modified-live vaccines may be contributing to the decline in their health, producing a condition known as vaccinosis. Some of the symptoms are cancer, low thyroid, autoimmune diseases, allergies, skin problems and temperament disorders. There is a growing number of veterinary articles and mounting evidence to support this. One alternative that is becoming available is a test for antibody titers. The duration of protection of any vaccine can be measured by this blood test, which is done to see what the animal's current immunity level is to certain diseases. That way, if a vaccination is required, one could be administered at that time. Dogs *must* have protection against diseases that would be fatal if contracted. However, there are an abundance of immunizations on the market today for nonfatal diseases. If the dog contracted the disease, he

The breeder went to great lengths to produce and care for your puppy until he became part of your family—it is now up to you to give him the best care you can. (Photo by Aubrey Abbott)

would recover and produce his own antibodies. For the future health of your puppy, make it your business not only to talk to your breeder and your veterinarian but also to do some reading and investigation of your own on the current protocols for vaccines recommended by the veterinarian research.

Distemper

Distemper is a highly contagious disease. It is similar to the measles virus in humans and is virtually incurable. It is most common in puppies from 3 to 8 months of age, but older dogs can get it, too. It is extremely important that your dog be vaccinated against this disease and that his vaccinations include those timed so that they would not have interfered with maternal antibodies. Distemper can be transmitted by other animals beside dogs such as squirrels, raccoons, foxes and wolves. Once a dog is exposed to the disease, the symptoms will usually start within three to fifteen days. Symptoms include a high fever of 103° to 105°, lethargy, loss of appetite and a watery discharge from the eyes and nose. Within a few days, the discharge will change from watery to thick. Eventually, this disease causes dehydration, brain damage and/or death. If your puppy develops any of these symptoms, get immediate veterinary attention.

Parvovirus

Parvovirus is an infectious disease that was first noted in the 1970s, and it is still prevalent today, unlike some of the other diseases that are almost nonexistent. With proper vaccinations at the right time, it can be a controllable disease. Puppies are highly susceptible to this disease, especially after the dam's immunity wears off and before they have had a chance to establish their own. This disease attacks bone marrow and the intestinal tract. Symptoms include vomiting, diarrhea and collapse. Immediate medical attention is needed to combat the dehydration and to start the correct therapy. High doses of vitamin C have been found to be effective in the treatment of this disease. Above all, if you have more than one dog in the house that has been exposed to this disease, do not run and vaccinate all your dogs against Parvo at this time. Their immune system will have already been compromised (not a good time to give an inoculation), and you may be at greater risk of losing the rest of them than the first dog that came down with the virus. Administer the same therapy to the rest of them that you are giving to the infected puppy for the best results.

Hepatitis

Canine hepatitis can be transmitted only to dogs. It is highly contagious and affects the liver, the kidneys and the lining of the blood vessels. Sometimes it is difficult to differentiate the disease from distemper. When the dog is exposed, the virus is shed in the saliva, stool and urine. A young puppy is the most susceptible during the first few months, but dogs of all ages can contract the disease. Symptoms include bloody diarrhea, high fever that can reach 106°F and jaundice.

Sometimes a dog will develop a clouding of the cornea of the eye or both eyes. This is called Blue Eye, and it can occur when a puppy is vaccinated for hepatitis as well. Although this doesn't happen often, it is something to be aware of.

Rabies

This is a fatal disease that is transmitted through the saliva of an infected animal, generally through a bite wound. This disease can occur in nearly all warm-blooded animals. The virus, which is in the saliva, infects any membrane it comes into contact with. The incubation period is usually two or three weeks. The virus moves to the brain where it causes inflammation (encephalitis). The symptoms exhibited are due to this inflammation and may at first only consist of personality changes. Your pet that used to be sociable will become aggressive and vicious. Pets that were not friendly before may become strangely affectionate. Soon they will want to withdraw completely and may stare into space. Other symptoms are vomiting, diarrhea and fever. Any wild animal that will let you get near it is not acting in a normal way and should be avoided. Watch your puppy when he is outdoors with you; take care that he is not approached by any other animals and that he does not run off to greet the squirrels. Talk to your breeder about when to vaccinate and keep the vaccination current for what is required by your state.

Bordetella (Kennel Cough)

The symptoms of this disease are coughing, retching and nasal discharge. This disease is highly contagious, can run through an entire kennel very quickly and lasts from a few days to several weeks. This disease is usually not life threatening, but if left untreated, the dog could develop broncho-pneumonia. Whether or not to vaccinate for this is up to the individual owner.

Coronavirus

This disease is pretty much self-limiting and has been known to mutate often, thereby making it difficult to produce a vaccine that will provide immunity to all strains. It was first noted, like Parvovirus, in the 1970s. Depression, vomiting and diarrhea as well as a yellow/brownish stool are some of the symptoms of this disease. Unless you live in an area that has a real problem with this, there should be no need to vaccinate against it.

Lyme Disease

This disease is named for the area in which the deer tick is located—Lyme, Connecticut—since this tick is the most common carrier of the disease. Symptoms include loss of appetite, fever, lameness and swelling of the joints. This vaccination is not highly recommended for toy breeds. Check with your veterinarian about the frequency of cases he may have treated in your area.

Leptospirosis

Leptospirosis is a disease caused by a bacteria called a *spirochete* that affects the functioning of the kidneys. This disease has been virtually eliminated in this country, and it is not a necessary vaccine for a Maltese. Many breeders have reported anaphylactic (allergic) reactions as mild as a rash and as severe as total collapse. Make sure your veterinarian knows about this before he administers a vaccine to your puppy. The leptospirosis part of the puppy series vaccine is the liquid and can be replaced with sterile water made for vaccines very easily.

Duration of Immunity

Research has indicated that some of the vaccines for these diseases have a lifetime duration of immunity. Distemper and Parvovirus are two that may fall into this category. Coronavirus and Rabies are the others. Some are questionable and may have a very poor duration. Kennel Cough vaccines and Lyme vaccines fall into that category. They may only last as long as six months to a year. The only way to really know whether your pet absolutely needs a vaccine is to do a titer test to check his immunity. If that is not a possibility, then a conservative approach to a vaccine schedule is probably the way to go. Talk to your veterinarian. If he is not willing to discuss with you your plan of action for your Maltese, find another veterinarian.

INTESTINAL PARASITES

Not all dogs with parasites will suffer from symptoms of a disease. If your puppy goes outside for any length of time, more than likely he will pick up worms sometime in his life. It is always wise to have your puppy's stool checked at the veterinarian to rule out the possibility of the existence of worms and be ahead of the game. A puppy can pick up worms running around outside, or he can be born with them. He can also develop a resistance to certain worms such as hookworms, roundworms and threadworms. Sometimes the worms can remain dormant in the dog's system until a stressful event (such as shipping a puppy) or trauma activates the larvae. Then you will start to see the parasites in the dog's stool. If the dam of your puppy's litter had dormant worms that did not show up on a stool sample inspected by your breeder's veterinarian, the stress of the pregnancy could activate the worms to travel to the unborn puppies. This does not mean your puppy was raised in bad or dirty circumstances. The best and most careful breeders can end up with a worm in their dog's stool. The solution is to take care of the

problem immediately and deworm the dog. Usually, after the dog is dewormed, he develops somewhat of an immunity that helps keep the worms in check later on.

Hookworms

Hookworms are small thin worms that are acquired when the dog contacts the larvae in contaminated soil or stools. The worms end up in the intestine and draw blood from the host. The eggs are passed in the stools. Unborn puppies can get hookworms while still inside their dam, and newborn puppies can get the worms from their dam's milk. Puppies have the potential to suffer more than adults from this parasite because of the anemia the worms cause. Tiny puppies can get sick and die quickly. Symptoms to watch for are weakness, diarrhea and weight loss. Always check with your veterinarian before administering any worming medication, especially to puppies. If your dog has had this type of worm, it is always good to have him periodically checked because this type of worm larvae can be dormant in the form of cysts in the dog's tissues. When the dog is stressed, there can be a new occurrence as the larvae become active again.

Even the prettiest and cleanest of puppies needs to be checked for the possibility of worms to avoid problems later on. (Photo by Vicki Abbott)

Tapeworms

Fleas are the most common cause of tapeworms. The flea gets the parasite by eating tapeworm eggs. The dog then bites the flea and swallows it, and the tapeworm eggs end up in the dog. Another way for the dog to get them is to eat a rat, rodent or other large game animal that has served as an intermediate host. Obviously, we would not expect any Maltese to be engaging in these activities. These worms live in the small intestine. The worms can be up to several feet in length. Segments of the worms, and/or their eggs, are passed in the stool. You will notice either the moving segments in the stool or possibly rice-like kernels around your dog's anus. These worms usually only cause a slight loss of appetite or mild diarrhea. It is fairly easy to rid your puppy or dog of these worms, and they can be controlled by controlling the flea population to which your dog is exposed (or his rat-chasing habits!).

Roundworms

These worms are acquired by your puppy or dog when he comes into contact with soil that contains the eggs. The eggs enter the mouth and end up in the intestines where they develop. Larvae are carried through the bloodstream, so if a dam has them, she can pass them along to her puppies. Puppies can also get them through nursing. Although these roundworms do not cause too much of a problem for an adult dog, they can be disastrous for a small puppy with a severe infestation. Symptoms are a potbellied appearance and a dull coat as well as vomiting, diarrhea and general failure to thrive. Unfortunately, worming the dam before or after the puppies are born does not help the puppies, so it is important to have the puppies checked. The worms appear like strands of

spaghetti or little white moving rice in the stool. Your veterinarian will prescribe the correct deworming for this situation according to the age of your dog.

Whipworms

The whipworm gets its name from its shape—thread-like but with one end thicker than the other. This worm is fairly hard to detect. Again, the dog will pick these up from egg-contaminated soil, and the worms will end up in the dog's intestines. Since they are not often passed in the stool, they are harder to diagnose. If your puppy is losing weight or has a constant diarrhea problem, have him checked for these as well as the other types of worms.

Coccidiosis and Giardiasis

These protozoan infections are usually found in young dogs. They can be acquired through feces, and puppies can reinfect themselves if they walk through their own stools. They can also acquire it from their mother. Symptoms include diarrhea, weight loss and lack of appetite. Sometimes there can also be a runny nose, a cough and eye discharge, which is similar to the symptoms of distemper. The first thing to do is stop the diarrhea to prevent the puppy from becoming dehydrated. Your veterinarian can prescribe a Kaopectate with an antibiotic, or you can buy Kaopectate over the counter at your drugstore. Kaopectate is a good remedy for diarrhea without any of the alcohol or salicylates that other products may contain.

There are drugs that are effective in the treatment of these protozoan diseases. Make sure you follow the veterinarian's instructions for the age of your puppy. Your puppy should be isolated from other dogs, and the yard or area in which the puppy relieves himself should be kept free of any feces.

Heartworm

This worm is spread by the common mosquito. Heartworm actually does reside in the heart. It also resides in the blood vessels of the lungs and can travel to the liver. The worms can number into the hundreds and can be 6 to 14 inches long. This is a life-threatening disease.

The dog acquires heartworm when bitten by an infected mosquito. The larvae work their way into the dog and into the bloodstream to develop into microfilariae. They progress to the heart where they mature. These worms interfere with the heart's ability to work. Some dogs can have these worms for years before you will notice any symptoms. Dogs with heartworm will exhibit symptoms of soft, deep coughing, like they cannot catch their breath. Later, the symptoms will resemble those of congestive heart failure. A heartworm test (a blood test to detect the microfilariae) must be performed by your veterinarian before your dog can be prescribed a preventative. He must be heartworm-free to take the medication. There are many safe preventatives on the market. If your dog is diagnosed with heartworms, the therapy must be strictly supervised because it is potentially dangerous and can cause heart failure. Obviously, the best way to avoid the problem is to have your puppy on heartworm preventative from the time he is old enough to do so, especially if you live in the South.

Heartworm is life-threatening and is spread by mosquitoes. If your dog spends time outside, especially in the South, he will need to be on heartworm-preventative medication. (Photo by Suzanne Johnston)

Hindsight is 20/20 Vision

Don't be an owner who should have done all these things to prevent these parasites from becoming a problem for your animal or one who never notices a problem until it is a little too late. Your Maltese has you to depend on and that's it. Your best chance of keeping your dog worm-free is to always properly pooper-scoop your yard. In addition, a fenced-in yard will keep out strays, and you should keep the yard clear of unwanted feces.

Do what you can to eliminate the possibility of mosquitoes around the house.

Take your puppy to the veterinarian for a stool check or just take the stool and have them check it for you. If the stool sample is found to be positive, give your puppy the appropriate medication prescribed by your veterinarian. After you have finished giving your puppy the medication, you will need to have the stool checked again to make sure he is worm-free. Usually, two negative samples over a period of time will be sufficient. Different types of worms may require different medications. If your puppy is diagnosed with more than one type, ask your veterinarian about the medications that will protect against more than one parasite at a time.

EXTERNAL PARASITES

Fleas

No Maltese puppy or dog should ever have to deal extensively with fleas. On a white dog, black

Fleas are a disaster for the Maltese with his luxurious white coat. Check on a regular basis to make sure your dog has not picked up some hitchhikers from the grass outdoors! (Photo by Vicki Abbott)

fleas are very easy to see and should be taken care of immediately. Flea bites can cause some severe allergies to the sensitive skin of a Maltese. The protein in the saliva of the flea is what causes this. Unfortunately, the cure is sometimes more harmful to the skin than the flea itself. Dips are usually too strong, can be toxic and tend to do more harm than good. Flea shampoos are usually not good for Maltese coats and do not work long-term. Flea collars are not very effective, and powders are definitely two thumbs down with all that hair! Make sure you obtain your flea products from your veterinarian. Avoid purchasing these from your local grocery or pet store. Pyrethrin- or permethrin-based products have been reported to cause problems in Maltese. Products that *will* work on a Maltese if he has a flea problem are the liquids Advantage and Frontline.

These solutions are placed on the dog's skin at the shoulder. They cannot be used on dogs used for breeding, but otherwise they are safe. Frontline comes in a pump spray that allows for easy application, and it is economical because it lasts for about three months. Sentinel, which contains an insect-growth inhibitor, has been shown to be a good oral control for heartworm and fleas for the Maltese. (Ivermectin has been observed to cause gastrointestinal problems in this breed.) Follow your veterinarian's instructions and the instructions on the medication.

If your Maltese picks up fleas somewhere, the best thing to do is bathe him immediately with his regular shampoo and conditioner. This will kill and rinse off the fleas. Then, after you have dried him, apply the liquid medication to the appropriate places to kill any flea eggs that might hatch or any fleas you may have missed. You will need to wash his bedding and anything he has been lying on. Treat the yard if that's where the puppy picked up the fleas. Ask your veterinarian about what products are safe to use around your puppy and read the labels carefully before treating any area. Adult fleas live on the dog, but flea eggs can drop off and contaminate the surrounding areas. If left untreated, these eggs will hatch and will jump back on the dog or, in the absence of the dog, even you! Both the eggs and the fleas themselves must be killed to stop the cycle. If there are any other pets in the house, they should be treated at the same time as your puppy or dog.

Since cats or other pets may require a different treatment, always consult your veterinarian before proceeding.

Ticks

A tick is a small flat insect, usually brown in color. There are several varieties of ticks, and all can possibly transmit disease. Rocky Mountain Spotted Fever, Lyme disease and encephalitis are a few of the diseases known to be transmitted by ticks. Some ticks can cause paralysis in dogs. Although the ticks usually start out very small, about the size of the head of a match, the female tick may puff up to the size of an eraser on the end of a pencil, or larger, when she has been feeding on the dog.

It is a good idea to check your dog periodically for fleas and ticks. Check for ticks around the dog's head, neck and ears as well as between his toes. If you find ticks on your dog, apply alcohol or clear fingernail polish directly to the tick. Get a tweezers and grab the dead tick as close to the skin as possible, using steady traction until it lets go. Try the best you can to get the head of the tick out with that first pull, but do not be concerned if the head remains in the skin. The most it may do is cause a mild reaction, which will go away in a few days. If you notice your dog developing any symptoms of illness or if the area does not clear up, contact your veterinarian for treatment.

Mange

There are three types of mange that we will mention here: demodectic, sarcoptic and cheyletiella. All three are itchy-skin disorders—not good for a Maltese!

Demodectic mange is a hair-loss disorder caused by a tiny mite, *Demodex Canis*. This mite is too small to be seen without the use of a microscope. It is a fact that most dogs have this mite living in their skin for their entire lives without the mite ever causing any symptoms. Puppies usually contract these mites from their mothers. If the dog's natural resistance to the mite is somehow compromised, the symptoms will start to be evident. In the early stages, this can start out looking like the dog is moth-eaten around the eyelids, mouth or front legs. As it advances, noticeable hair loss in patches occurs around the head, legs and body, and sores will begin to form. If you suspect your dog may have mange, you must get him to the veterinarian so he can do a skin scraping. This will not hurt the dog or puppy. Your veterinarian can then look at the scraping under the microscope to detect the mites and prescribe treatment, which will usually be in the form of an ointment or lotion such as Goodwinol. Puppies usually suffer the most from this, but an adult dog that has been through a lot of stress or that has a compromised immune system can also have this problem.

Sarcoptic mange, or **scabies**, is a most intense form of skin disorder. It will cause your dog to scratch and bite at himself vigorously. This type of mange is also caused by mites that must be diagnosed by a skin scraping under the microscope. In the case of scabies, the mites tunnel into the dog's skin to lay their eggs, which is what causes the intense itching. The first signs of this problem are little red bumps that appear to be insect bites. As the dog scratches, the area becomes like a sore—crusty and with scabs. You will also notice that the hair is gone in patches. These mites are highly contagious to other dogs and can be transferred to you, although they do not live long on humans. Check for this type of mange on the skin of the ears, elbows, legs and face of your dog. Insecticide dips have proven effective in killing these mites, but certain dips may be more toxic than others to small dogs. Therefore, treatment for this type of mange should be supervised by your veterinarian.

Cheyletiella mange is called **walking dandruff** because you will recognize this problem by the appearance of dandruff over the dog's head, neck and back. This is also a mite, but it lives on the surface of the skin and will die shortly after falling off the dog. Your veterinarian will diagnose this mite with a skin scraping. Since walking dandruff is also highly contagious, it should be treated immediately. Treatment for this type of mange is the same as for sarcoptic mange.

ALLERGIES

A Maltese can become allergic to something in his surroundings or to an ingredient in the food he is eating. He can be allergic to certain parts of a vaccine. The allergy can be from something the dog inhales or something he contacts. They are two different types of allergy. To determine if your puppy might have a predisposition for some of these types of allergies, it is a good idea to talk with your

Certain plants can be poisonous, and some can cause aller-gies. Make sure all houseplants are out of reach of your Maltese and ask your veterinarian about any plants if your dog seems to have an allergy to something. (Photo by Catherine Lawrence)

breeder about the possibility of a history of allergies among his relatives. Allergies do not always run in families, however. If your puppy seems to be scratching or there is redness of the skin, this might signal an allergy. Sometimes the dog's eyes will water and stain because of an allergy you might not be aware of. Ask your veterinarian about a blood test that will tell you what your Maltese may be allergic to. Then you can begin the process of eliminating whatever may be the cause. Your veterinarian may also prescribe cortisone for your dog, a drug that can be helpful to stop the itching and scratching and to allow the skin to heal.

THYROID DYSFUNCTION

This is a condition that sometimes affects Maltese and is easy to treat. If the thyroid gland is not putting out enough thyroid hormone, this deficiency is called *hypothyroidism.* When a Maltese has this condition, his coat can become thin and brittle. He may become obese and lethargic. Breeders will notice this more readily because it produces irregular heat cycles. To diagnose this condition, a blood test will be run by your veterinarian to check the thyroid levels. If the diagnosis is hypothyroidism, it is easy to treat with a thyroid hormone in the form a small pill daily.

THE CANINE LIVER

Recently, within the past ten years or so, there has been much research involving the canine liver. One of the problems that can be a possibility in Maltese, as well as other toy breeds, is a liver malformation call a *portosystemic shunt.* This is a congenital malformation of the veins that take blood through the liver. Congenital means that the condition existed at birth but was not necessarily hereditary. The job of the liver is to process any impurities out of the blood. If the veins are malformed and bypass the liver for this process, blood is sent to the other vital parts of the body without being detoxified.

Puppies that have this abnormality will usually not thrive and are at their worst right after eating. However, some dogs can live with this condition for many years, and the problem may go undiagnosed until they start to show symptoms. The screening test currently offered for this condition is called a Serum Bile Acid Test. A blood test is taken after the dog has fasted for twelve hours. The dog is then fed, and the blood is retested after another couple of hours. This test will show the liver's ability to clear bile acids. An abnormality will indicate that there is some type of dysfunction. However, this can only *suggest* that there *might* be a shunt, and the tests on Maltese have been known to show some false positives for liver dysfunction.

Signs that might indicate your Maltese needs to be tested are neurological problems such as weakness, seizures, stumbling or excessive sleepiness, stones in the urinary bladder or poor weight gain. If your Maltese is diagnosed with this problem, make sure you get a second opinion because there are other conditions a Maltese may have that would produce similar symptoms. Unfortunately, the only current way to definitely diagnose a liver shunt is to do exploratory surgery. The research that is ongoing will hopefully produce another way for the Maltese owner to know for sure what the situation really is before deciding to put the dog through that type of an operation.

ALTERNATIVE THERAPY

Homeopathy is a system of medicine that was formalized by a German physician, Samuel Hahnemann, in the early 1900s. Although homeopathy fell out of favor in the United States in the early twentieth century, it has developed a resurgence in this country over the last few years. People are looking for safe alternatives for many chronic diseases that are difficult to treat such as viral infections, allergies and autoimmune disorders.

Many veterinarians are trained in both orthodox and homeopathic medicine. Holistic therapies are a proven alternative to the standard medical approach. Obviously, in this day and time, we are

Suzanne and Dolly share a very special connection. The health of your Maltese can be greatly affected by the love and attention he receives. (Photo by Linda Lamoureux)

more aware of what we are putting into our bodies and how it is affecting us. We should be aware of the same things when it concerns our pets. A holistic approach to medicine is a natural one, dealing with nutrition and overall health. If you feel this might be something you would be interested in for your pet, you can probably find these specialized veterinarians in the telephone directory or over the Internet. Information pertaining to this can also be found in Appendix A of this book.

THE COMMONSENSE APPROACH

We have attempted to point out some of the things your Maltese could possibly have a problem with during his lifetime. Obviously, we cannot cover everything you might be faced with in the way of medical problems. Much of your dog's health depends on prevention. The diseases that can be fatal should be controlled by vaccination. Parasites can be prevented by taking care of your surroundings and by applying prescribed medications. Your puppy should receive an annual checkup, not for additional vaccinations but to prevent any problems or to catch them in the early stages.

There are many problems your dog may encounter in his lifetime that are not under your or your breeder's control. These problems may be congenital, or your dog may be predisposed to the problem. Still, proper grooming and commonsense care will enhance the life of your Maltese.

Here are some tips to ensure that you have a happy, healthy Maltese:

- Know how to get in touch with your veterinarian if there is an emergency and what 24-hour emergency clinic he recommends. Just being able to make a phone call to ask a question about symptoms and what to do for them can keep you from staying up all night.

Proper grooming plays a big part in keeping your Maltese healthy. (Photo by Pamela Rightmyer)

- If your dog has a fever, you will want to contact the doctor because this is a sign of infection.

- Vomiting and diarrhea are not emergencies unless the dog also has a high fever or other symptoms that might suggest an illness. Sometimes puppies just have an upset stomach. This can be treated with Kaopectate or another antidiarrhea product that your veterinarian recommends. Dehydration is what you want to avoid, so make sure your dog drinks plenty of water. Medication or water can be given to a dog in a syringe with the needle removed. Just squirt the liquid into his mouth.

- Know the eating habits of your dog. If he goes off his food for one meal, it may not be a problem; but if he does not seem to want to eat for more than a day, contact your veterinarian for advice.

CHAPTER SEVEN

Routine Care for the Maltese

It is likely that the majority of dogs live in a family environment. The companionship they provide is well worth the work involved. Care of your Maltese will be enjoyable time spent developing a relationship between you and your dog. The Maltese needs that extra attention he gets while you go about taking care of his needs.

NUTRITION—WHAT TO FEED

Food Additives

It is very critical that you read and understand what is in your dog's food. All the ingredients are listed on the label. For instance, if chicken is the primary ingredient in the bag of food, it will be listed first and so on. Unless the company adds the ingredient at the point of manufacturing, they are not required to list it on the label. So what do you do? You find a reputable dog-food company that states on the label that there are no toxic ingredients such as those we are going to talk about.

Many new dog foods are highly recommended by breeders and veterinarians alike. We like to call them "premium brands." Some of these foods are Innova, Pet Guard, Wyssong, California Natural, Halo

Vicki's daughter Aubrey has, for years, played a big role in socializing each and every Maltese. Handling from an early age will help a Maltese puppy grow up to be well-adjusted. (Photo by Vicki Abbott)

Diets, Precise and Flint River Ranch. Some of these foods are even oven baked to keep in the most nutrients possible. Talk to your puppy's breeder about what his dogs are fed. It is always a good idea to keep your puppy on whatever the breeder suggests for at least a while after you bring

him home. If you wish to change to a different food, you can start by gradually mixing the new food into the food you have already been feeding until you have changed over completely.

Studies have shown that certain preservatives used in dog and cat foods can be dangerous to our animals. (Preservatives are used to prevent the food from going rancid.) These preservatives include ethoxyquin, BHA and BHT. If the ingredient, such as the meat, already has one of these preservatives in it before it is added to the food, it will probably not be listed on the label. BHA and BHT can cause allergic reactions and can affect the liver and kidney functions. Ethoxyquin was first used in making tires as a rubber stabilizer. When this was introduced as a preservative, many pet owners started noticing new occurrences of all kinds of conditions in their animals. Research has established that these types of preservatives are definitely not good for the long-term good health of your dog and may, in fact, produce cancers and other problems. Look for a food that contains natural preservatives such as vitamins E and C, which are used in the "premium brands."

Meat should be the number one ingredient in the food you choose. Look at the meat source on the label and make sure there are no byproducts, bone meal or digest. There are many different types of meat in dog foods. Those you will usually find in good foods are lamb, chicken or beef. If your Maltese has developed an allergy of some sort, you might want to check to see if the food he is eating is the cause. Some Maltese can be allergic to poultry products, and most food allergies in dogs are related to the protein they are eating.

Supplements can aid in your dog's digestion, skin and coat condition and overall health. (Photo by Noreen Bieniek & Expressly Portraits)

Supplements

We recommend that you supplement your dog's food. There are many supplements on the market for your Maltese. Most dog foods are cooked, removing valuable vitamins. There is a supplement called Missing Link that we wholeheartedly recommend. It not only contains vitamins but also many things that will aid in your dog's digestion and overall health. There are a number of good books on nutrition that we will list for you in the Bibliography.

Water

Drinking water can be a problem without you even realizing it. There are many things added to our city drinking water and things that are not

purified out. If your Maltese seems to have more facial stain than is normal, and you have ruled out everything else you can think of, consider buying purified, bottled drinking water for awhile. This will help you determine whether the minerals or additives in your water are changing the color of the tears on your Maltese or are causing a slight allergic reaction.

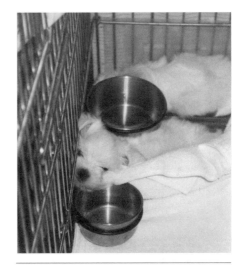

Make sure the water you give your puppy is purified and free from chemicals or harsh minerals, which can promote facial staining and possibly be toxic. (Photo by Vicki Abbott)

THE FEEDING SCHEDULE

A schedule for your puppy's feedings should be established and adhered to strictly because this will aid you in housetraining him effectively. Stick to the breeder's schedule for the number of times a day the puppy needs to be fed. A younger puppy will eat more often than an adult, probably three or four times a day. As he gets older, these feeding times will decrease. The following is a suggested schedule:

1. Take the puppy outside first thing in the morning, praising him when he relieves himself in the appropriate place.

2. Feed the puppy his morning meal and then let him out once again.

3. Between noon and 2pm, take the puppy out—he will need to go by now. (Feed him a noon meal if required.)

4. When you arrive home from work or in the early evening, take the puppy out before you feed him.

5. Bring the puppy back in and feed him his evening meal.

6. Take the puppy out after he eats and once again before bedtime.

7. Remember to keep the puppy confined when he cannot be watched or supervised. Always praise him when he relieves himself in the appropriate place.

Maltese generally are the type of eaters that like to eat a little and then come back for the rest later. If you must go to work during the day, we suggest that you leave the food in the bowl for your puppy to finish. It will be gone by the time you get home. Leave fresh water available and leave some papers or hospital pads on the floor for the puppy in case he needs to go while you are away.

Do not feed your puppy table scraps. When fed a good diet, he will have all the good food he needs to maintain a healthy life. We sometimes tend to try to put our feelings into the dog and wonder whether they'd like more of a variety or more colorful food. Since it has not been proven that dogs even see color, this argument does not make sense. They eat when they are hungry and probably don't remember what they had for lunch! If you are feeding good, nutritious food, the puppy will like it. Introducing all kinds of different foods can unbalance a dog's diet and cause obesity.

EXERCISE

A Maltese is a very active dog, and he will exercise himself without you having to put him on any kind of exercise program. You can take your puppy or dog on short walks if you like, as this will give him fresh air and sunshine. Try not to overdo it with a very young puppy because his bones are still growing and you don't want to stress his body or encourage any structural damage. You can extend the walks the closer to a year old he gets; by then, he will be more mature.

Maltese love recreational activities that include playing with them. Tossing a ball so your dog can retrieve it does not require good weather or a great amount of space. If your Maltese tends to be obese or lethargic, there may be another problem that requires veterinary attention, not exercise. Normal Maltese behavior is playful, and they are happy to go wherever you do!

This was the cute picture on one of Sandra Kenner and Chris Pearson's Christmas cards. Is this how a Maltese from Colorado exercises?

EQUIPMENT FOR ROUTINE CARE

Caring for your dog's routine needs can prevent the need for medical attention and can prolong his life. You will need to have certain grooming tools for the routine care of your Maltese. You need a small pair of nail scissors for clipping the nails. A pair of small, straight scissors is needed to trim the hair off the toe pads. You need a tooth scaler, a toothbrush, good dog toothpaste and possibly some dog tooth-cleaning pads. Add to your kit some eye ointment, ear-cleaning solution, hydrogen peroxide, Kwik Stop (to stop any bleeding

from clipped nails), Panalog (a general antibiotic ointment) and Kaopectate or other antidiarrhea medication recommended by your veterinarian. Your veterinarian may also be able to provide you with a small supply of general antibiotics to keep on hand in case of an emergency. Cotton-tipped swabs, cotton balls and antibacterial soap should also be among the items in your routine-care kit.

MALTESE EARS

A dog's ears are important to him because his hearing is one of his best senses. Dogs can hear things we cannot. They rely on their hearing to let them know what is around them.

The inside of a Maltese ear should be nice and pink. A small amount of wax in the ears, which will be light brown in color, is normal and helps keep the tissues healthy. Before starting to clean the ear, put some ear-cleansing solution into the ear and massage it from the outside to loosen any dirt. Do not use alcohol or other irritating solutions. They are not good for the ear and may even be painful to the dog.

Using a cotton ball or a clean cloth, wipe the entrance to the ear canal and the skin surface of the ear. You can then use a cotton swab to gently clean out the ear canal. The dog's ear canal drops vertically on the inside and then turns to continue horizontally. When cleaning your dog's ears, hold the swab at a vertical angle and downwards. This will eliminate the possibility of damage to the eardrum. You might put a little mineral oil on the swab before doing this. Even though the Maltese has a drop ear, folded over like a spaniel, he probably will not need to have his ears cleaned very often. Sporting dogs with drop ears that hunt around water and dogs that go swimming are more susceptible to bacteria forming in their ears because water can get trapped in the ear canal. When you give your Maltese a bath, make sure no water gets into his ears. You can put cotton in them to prevent this. Make sure that, when you blow dry your Maltese, the insides of his ears are dry, too.

If you take your Maltese to a professional groomer, help the groomer understand that he should not pluck the excess hair out of your dog's ears. When this is done it make the pores ooze, and an infection can occur. If you need to pull any hair out of the ears, for instance, if it gets too thick or matted, gently pluck a few hairs at a time with either a small forceps or tweezers. Then apply antibiotic ointment such as Panalog to the ear canal. Massage the ear on the outside to spread the ointment around inside the ear. This will prevent the open pores from becoming infected.

If the inside of your dog's ear becomes very red or swollen or there is dark brown discharge, you will need to take your dog to the veterinarian. Your Maltese may have a bacterial infection or a fungus infection, or he may have ear mites. A trip to the doctor will identify what the problem is so it can be treated correctly, as different medications will be prescribed for each of these problems.

Ear medications for dogs usually come in a tube with a long nozzle on the end. To apply medication to the ear of your dog, take the tube and insert the nozzle into the ear canal downward. Hold the dog's head with your other hand so he will not jerk away and cause damage to his ear.

Squeeze a few drops of the medication into the ear and remove the tube. You will need to get the medicine all the way into the canal, so massage the ear at the base on the outside gently—this will make a squishy sound, and you will know the medication is moving around in his ear where you want it.

When you bring your puppy home, you should test his hearing. Dogs can be born without the ability to hear. This can be congenital (from birth), or the loss can occur later on in life from trauma, infection or old age. A dog that is going

The best place for your Maltese to be during routine care is on the grooming table, where you can sit and face the dog while you are taking care of his eyes or ears. (Photo by Vicki Abbott)

deaf may not show the symptoms immediately. If your dog is difficult to arouse from sleep, seems to ignore you more than usual or his voice seems to change, you should probably have him examined. Puppies are usually so active that it is difficult to tell whether they cannot hear until you get them all by themselves. You can then blow a whistle or make a sound behind the puppy's back to see if he responds.

MALTESE EYES

Maltese eyes should be dark and clear. There is really no routine care of the eyes unless a problem is noticed.

Problems with your dog's eyes might include injury or excessive tearing. If your dog has scratched the surface of his eye or has run into something that has caused an injury, you must be careful not to administer anything with a cortisone in it because this will cause permanent scarring. The best plan of action is to get to the vet-erinarian as soon as possi-ble. He will then prescribe the correct medication, probably in the form of an ointment, to heal the injury.

The lovely eyes of a Maltese should be dark and clear with no clouding or redness. (Photo by Christine Pearson & Sandra Kenner)

above the eye. Pulling up gently with your left thumb and down with your right, you can examine the eye quick-ly. If there is no injury that you can detect, he may just have irritated eyes. The reasons for this could be any number of things. He could be allergic to something. He could have had a foreign substance in his eye that is now gone. Hair could be getting into his eyes and irritat-ing them. If you are using your fireplace or you smoke, the smoke can be very irritating to Maltese eyes. Or he could have an eye infec-tion. It is always good to have on hand some soothing or antibiotic

If your dog has an eye irritation or he is rub-bing his eyes, first check for any injury that might be present. You can do this by examining the eye-ball under the light. With your Maltese on the grooming table, hold his head in your hands. Take your right thumb and place it just below your dog's eye. Place your left thumb on the bone just

eye drops. These can be purchased from your vet-erinarian. Lubricating drops or ointment made for people are also good for dogs and can be obtained from your local market in the pharmacy section where the eye and contacts solutions are found. Treat your dog's eyes with antibiotic eye drops or ointment for 24 hours. If there is no improve-ment, call your veterinarian.

Minor eye problems can develop into some-thing much worse, so do not ignore them hoping they will just clear up on their own. Apply eye drops directly to your dog's eyeball. Pull up gently on the upper lid and, holding the bottle over the eye so it does not actually touch the eyeball, squeeze two or three drops onto the eyeball and close the eye. Ointment is applied to the inner surface of the lower eyelid. You can accomplish this by placing your finger on the dog's cheek below the eye and pulling down gently as you squeeze a little ointment into the lower eyelid.

Conjunctivitis

When the lining on the inside of the eye is inflamed and there is an obvious discharge, this is called conjunctivitis. If the discharge gets to the point of being pus-filled or crusty, there is probably a bacterial infection present. Cleansing the eye often and administering specific antibiotics for the infection will usually clear this up. A culture done by your veterinarian may be required to identify the bacteria and to prescribe the correct medication.

Watery Eyes or Tearing

There is no doubt that, if you own a Maltese, you will be faced with this problem sometime in his life. The hair on a Maltese, especially as a puppy, does tend to get into the eyes and irritate them. Maltese also can be sensitive to certain things or have allergies, and their eyes may become red and watery. However, there is a difference between the normal tearing of the eyes of a Maltese for lubrication and to keep them free from foreign substances and a problem that needs medical attention.

Finding the cause of the tearing and stains on your Maltese is a process of elimination.

- **Tear Drainage:** Dogs can have a condition in which the tears they produce are not adequately drained. The tears usually overflow onto the face because there is some kind of obstruction or blockage in the normal drainage system. This can be caused by a number of things. The ducts themselves may be blocked or not exist due to a birth defect. The ducts can be scarred after an infection or narrowed for some reason. Your veterinarian can test for blockage of the ducts by staining the tears with a dye. If the dye ends up at the nostril of the dog, the tear duct is open. If not, the duct can possibly be flushed out.

- **Chronic Tonsillitis:** Infections of the throat can be very low grade and hardly noticeable to the owner. A dog can have a chronic case of tonsillitis that, over time, can cause scarring of the ducts or just keep the eyes tearing. Have your veterinarian check your dog's throat and take his temperature to see if there are any indications of a mild infection that may need a course of antibiotics.

- **Chronic Ear Infection:** Sometimes a dog can also have a slight ear infection that will cause the eyes to react by draining. Indication of infection is usually a rise in temperature but not always.

- **Eye Damage or Allergy:** If there is an injury to the eye or if the dog is allergic to something, there will be more tearing than usual. Rule out any eye injury. If allergies are suspected, have your Maltese tested with a blood test to see what the dog is allergic to. It may be as simple as changing his food. However, many dogs are allergic to the same pollens that we are. If the problem is air born, you may be able to put your dog on a program of allergy shots that will eliminate the symptoms.

• **Eye Damaging Behavior:** Things that dogs can do to damage themselves are endless, but you can control most of them. Do not let your dog hang his head out of the window of a car while it is moving; this will obviously expose his eyes to fast-moving foreign objects. There are some dogs that just have to rub their head and eyes on anything in sight. This is not a good behavior for a Maltese to get into the habit of doing. Watch your dog for any behavior that might be the cause of his red eyes, and put a stop to it when it happens!

When you have ruled out everything that you think might be the cause of the excess tearing and stains, you will be right where almost every Maltese breeder and exhibitor has been before. What is the answer to the brown stains on your Maltese? Tetracycline has provided an answer for some because it seems to bind the tears that stain the face. The face may still be damp but not discolored. Talk to your veterinarian about a course of tetracycline for about three to four weeks. (Puppies cannot be given tetracycline until their permanent teeth come in.) If this does not help permanently, you may need to administer it again or try another antibiotic. Talk to the breeder of your puppy or dog. There are many alternatives that have worked within particular lines of dogs. Cosmetically, you can apply dry cornstarch directly to the whiskers

of the Maltese on a daily basis. Once the cornstarch is applied to the stained area, take a cloth and press it into the hair. Then take a fine-toothed comb and comb through the hair, leaving in as much cornstarch as you can without it being clumpy. Over a period of time, this can lighten the stain.

Cloudy Eye and Blue Eye

Cloudy eye is exactly the way it sounds. If for some reason you start to notice that the cornea of your dog's eye is becoming dull or milky in color, take him to the vet. This is called keratitis and can be caused by injury or infection. It could lead to partial or total blindness and is always serious.

Blue eye is when a bluish-white film forms over the dog's eye. This condition is usually caused by the hepatitis virus. It can be caused by the disease itself or by a hepatitis vaccination.

Cataracts

When the lens of your dog's eye loses its transparency, he probably has cataracts. This can be in the form of a very small spot or can cover the eye completely. Cataracts are common in older dogs. If the cataract causes your dog's vision to be impaired so much that he cannot get around very easily, you may want to consider having it removed surgically.

THE MOUTH AND TEETH

Ignoring the dental health of your Maltese can shorten his life. Therefore, it is extremely important that you provide the correct care for your dog's teeth at all stages. When you acquire your puppy, he will probably have his baby, or deciduous, teeth. They begin to appear at about 3 or 4 weeks old and are finished erupting at about 6 weeks of age. Bigger dogs will get all their teeth earlier than the smaller breeds. There are twenty-eight deciduous teeth in a puppy. They consist of the canines (long and pointed), the incisors (front teeth) and the pre-molars (back of the mouth).

At about 4 months of age, puppies begin shedding their baby teeth. In toy breeds, these teeth often need some help to come out to make way for the permanent teeth. The smaller incisors will come out first, and then the canine teeth erupt. When the puppy tooth does not come out before the permanent one erupts, it is called a *retained tooth*. These retained teeth can make it impossible for the permanent ones to come in correctly, and it can cause the bite on your dog to be incorrect.

Incorrect bites can cause many problems including gum infections and pain. It is a good idea to check your puppy's mouth periodically to make sure his baby teeth are coming out and the permanents are coming in correctly. A visit to the veterinarian may be in order to pull a few retained baby teeth for the overall future health of your dog.

Puppies begin to chew on things as part of their physical and mental development. Not only are they exploring, they are also loosening those baby teeth to help them come out. Provide safe and adequate chew toys for your puppy during this time.

There are toys made out of rope that have a flossing action on the teeth of your puppy. These are made with the safety of your dog in mind. They are durable chew products. Some of them have raised places on the surface that help to clean the teeth. These chew toys will massage the gums of your puppy or dog as he chews, increasing the circulation to the gums.

The correct bite for a Maltese is either scissors or even. The scissors bite is ideal for dental health. The even bite, while acceptable, is less ideal because the constant contact of the teeth in this kind of a bite will wear them down. Bad bites can be common problems for toy breeds because their mouths are very small. A lot of times the reason a really great dog will be sold is because his bite is a little off. This can be because the baby teeth didn't come out on time or because of heredity. Either way, a wonderfully bred puppy with a not-so-perfect bite is a great find as a pet. This will not affect the puppy's overall health as long as you take care of his teeth.

The normal number of teeth for the adult dog is forty-two. Examine your dog's mouth on a weekly basis throughout his first year to make sure there are no sores, foreign objects or tooth problems. When all the permanent teeth are in, the buildup of tartar will start. This can lead to gum disease and tooth loss. Regular cleanings will keep your dog's teeth and gums healthy.

Teach your puppy early to allow you into his mouth without struggling. Start with short looks and then lengthen them until he lets you touch his teeth. There are several products on the market to aid you in keeping your dog's teeth clean until the time comes for more aggressive measures. The tooth scaler will help knock some of the built-up tartar off the teeth.

Most of the tartar will probably accumulate on the back molars to begin with. Care must be taken not to cut or injure the gums while you are scraping this off. This must be started early, or the dog will never let you get into his mouth to do this. A small toothbrush and dog toothpaste can be used to help prevent decay of the teeth and to keep the surfaces slick, thereby preventing tartar buildup. Do not use human toothpaste on your dog. Dog toothpaste can be found at your veterinarian or

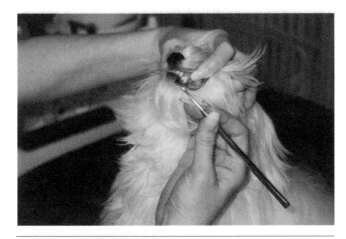

If you teach your Maltese early to let you work with his mouth, you will have more success with dental maintenance later on. Here, a tooth scaler is used to knock off the tartar. This should not take the place of regular cleaning by the veterinarian. (Photo by Larry Abbott)

pet-supply store. You can also purchase packages of small, disposable cloths that you wrap around your finger to rub on your dog's teeth to clean them.

By the time most dogs are 4 years old, 75% of them have periodontal disease. This is the most common infection in dogs. When you are no longer successful at being able to remove most of the tartar, or if your dog will not let you do this maintenance in his mouth, it will be time for your veterinarian to do a prophylactic cleaning. To do this thorough cleaning, it will be necessary to put your dog under anesthesia. With modern gas anesthetics and monitoring equipment, this procedure is fairly safe. Talk to your veterinarian about his procedures. Some cities have veterinary dental specialists where you can take your dog for his dental health care.

The veterinarian will scale the teeth with an ultrasound scaler or a hand instrument, somewhat like what you go through at the dentist's office. If there are problems below the gum line, he will plane the roots to make them smooth. If a tooth is infected or needs to be pulled, he will take care of this by packing it with antibiotics or removing it properly. Discuss with your veterinarian the possibilities of what might have to be done before the cleaning so there are no surprises. It is not the end of the world if a tooth has to be pulled on an older dog. He can eat very well without it, and it may end up improving his overall health to get rid of the problem and the infection.

Cleaning may become more frequent as your dog gets older. Talk with your veterinarian about any tests he might want to do before administering anesthesia. The organs such as the heart, liver and kidney on geriatric patients do not function as well as when they were young.

TRIMMING MALTESE NAILS

This is a regular maintenance that you need to do about every four to six weeks. Your puppy should be used to having his nails trimmed when you acquire him. Ask the breeder how he trimmed the nails on your puppy. The easiest way to trim nails is with the dog on his back in your lap. You should train your young puppy to do this because it is a position you will need for him to be in for grooming as well. Maltese nails can be either white or black. It is next to impossible to see the quick (the thin vein that runs down the middle of the nail) on nails that are black, but it is fairly easy on the white ones. The quick will appear to be a pinkish color. Black and white nails can be on the same dog. Start out by purchasing the correct type of nail trimmer. The scissors type is much preferred by the dogs over the guillotine type. The guillotine type of trimmer makes a slight noise or squeak right before it gets to the nail. This tends to make the dogs jump, and they get tuned in to pull away just as you are about to trim the nail. The scissors type is quiet, and you can position it where you want it on the nail better.

Position the nail trimmer right below the quick so you do not cut into it. Usually this will be about where the nail starts to curve. If you do accidentally cut into the quick a little, do not panic. We don't think any dog has ever bled to death from a nick to his nail. Apply a product called Kwik Stop, which will stop the bleeding. This is a yellow powder, and you can dip the dog's nail into it. It should stop the bleeding very quickly.

Do all the nails on one foot at a time. Do not forget to look for dew claws, which may or may not have been removed by the breeder's veterinarian. The dew claw is a nail on the side of the foot. Most Maltese only have them on their front feet. Depending on the size or the health of the puppies at 3 days of age, a breeder makes his own decision. The standard does not require the removal of these, and you can't see them under the hair anyway. It's just good to know whether they are there because they have to be trimmed just like a nail. If left untrimmed, they can get so long that they curl around and pierce the skin.

After you have trimmed all the toenails, it is time to trim the hair from the toe pads.

A pair of small, straight scissors is good for this. Hair must be kept trimmed away from the toe pads to prevent the toes from splaying, or being pushed apart. Very carefully, so as not to cut the pad in any way, trim the hair around the pads. There is no need to dig way between the toes. Just trim it to the level of the foot, and make sure you can see all the pads. This will also give your dog better traction on slick surfaces because overgrown hair on the foot will make him slide.

Deformation of your dog's foot can occur if proper care is not taken to trim the nails on a regular basis. This is one of the easier parts of the routine care of your Maltese. Mark on the calendar when you last trimmed them or keep an eye on how long they are getting and trim them accordingly.

ANAL GLANDS

The anal glands on a dog are located on either side of the anus. They are sacks that accumulate secretions that need to be drained periodically. Groomers will usually do this before they bathe a dog. If your dog is groomed at a shop, you may want to ask the groomer to do this. However, unpleasant as this may sound, it is fairly easy to do on your own dog, and you will absolutely know that it was done and done correctly. Dogs with full anal sacks will sometimes scoot across the floor to try to relieve the pressure. The best time to express the anal glands is in the sink or tub right before you give your dog a bath. Use a paper towel in doing this; the liquid expressed does not have the nicest smell, and it can come out with some force.

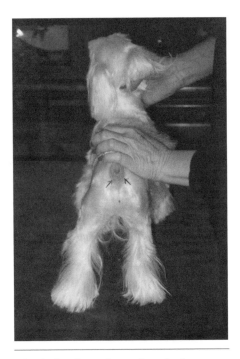

Anal glands are located on the lower sides of the anal opening and need to be expressed occasionally to prevent them from becoming impacted. (Photo by Larry Abbott)

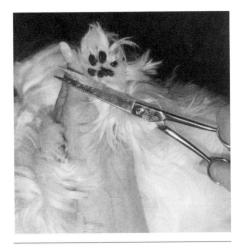

After clipping the toenails, trim the hair away from the toe pads carefully with a small scissors so you can see each one. (Photo by Larry Abbott)

Apply gentle pressure to both sides of the anal opening. Do not squeeze too hard because this can injure the dog. If this is done on a regular basis, it will prevent the glands from becoming plugged up, or impacted, which requires veterinary attention. After this is done, you can bathe the dog, eliminating any odor or residue from the anal glands.

(Photo by Taylor Taylor, Mariko Sukezaki & Vicki Abbott)

CHAPTER EIGHT

Grooming Your Maltese

There is not another toy dog that possesses the long, white, sparkling hair that makes a Maltese so attractive. When you decided on this breed, it was probably one of the first things you liked so much. To keep a Maltese coat, you must be willing to take the time to brush and bathe your dog on a regular basis. This is not a breed you can let go for days and expect the coat to take care of itself. If you let the coat get extremely matted, your dog's skin will not be able to breathe, and you will have to shave the hair off and start over again. In addition to this not being attractive, it is not good for the dog. When the hair is matted to the skin, it is extremely hard to shave it without getting too close to the skin and causing irritation or even razor burns. If brushing hair is not for you, why not get a smooth-coated breed instead?

THE PET COAT

You can groom your own Maltese. The breeder from whom you acquired your puppy has probably already started his grooming routine, so he may be accustomed to being brushed. You will continue with these grooming sessions, starting with the day you bring your puppy home.

Your first piece of grooming equipment should be a grooming table with a nonskid surface. This can be purchased at most any pet store. Ask your breeder where he purchased the one he has. If you can't find a grooming table, any sturdy table with a nonskid pad will be fine as long as it does not wobble and scare the dog. Attempting to groom the dog on the floor or anywhere other than a table will only create frustration. The puppy will probably attempt to get away from you when he decides he's had enough, and

Mirror, mirror, there's nothing prettier than a beautifully groomed Maltese! (Photo by Connie Phillips & Roberta Werner)

Invest in a good dog shampoo and conditioner. These should be recommended by your breeder or someone who has some knowledge of how to groom the breed. Many whitening shampoos are too harsh for the Maltese coat. Do not just use a human baby shampoo thinking it will be mild. This will dry out Maltese hair. There has been much research that has produced some excellent shampoos to use on our Maltese. The pH of a dog's hair is different from that of a human, so the correct shampoos must be used to keep the hair in optimum condition. This will also make it easier on you because the coat will mat less between baths.

Begin your puppy's training by laying him down on his side on the table. Reassure him

you will spend most of your time chasing him around the room!

Another item you will need is a good dog dryer. Purchase a dryer on a stand that allows you to have both of your hands free for grooming the dog. Other items to add to your grooming kit are a couple of good pin brushes, a steel comb and a ratting comb. The steel comb should have a fine-tooth end and a larger-tooth end. The ratting comb can be found at any beauty supply store. It has a fine-tooth plastic comb on one end and a metal hair parter on the other end. The pin brushes can be found at a dog-supply store that sells supplies for show dogs. These items should be of good quality to last you for a long time. You should never use what is called a *slicker brush* on a Maltese. This can cause severe damage to the coat.

Arisa is groomed and sitting pretty on a pad on top of the sink. (Photo by Mariko Sukezaki)

that he is a good dog and that he should stay on his side. Do this a number of times before you attempt to brush him. When you start with your new puppy, he will not have a lot of coat to deal with, so teaching him the proper behavior on the table will save you much time as the coat grows longer.

Begin brushing the puppy coat with a pin brush. Turn your puppy on his back in your lap while you are sitting in a chair in front of your grooming table. Brush through the coat on his tummy and legs. Then use your steel comb to gently go back through the hair so you will be sure you did not miss any tangles or mats. If you hit a tangle, do not pull it out forcefully. Instead, kind of work it out with the comb a little at a time. You will lose less hair this way. Be careful around his back legs because the bones are thin in places and can catch on the comb. Also be careful with the brush and comb around his private parts. Make sure there are no mats under his front legs, as Maltese tend to mat pretty badly in that area.

Now turn the puppy over and either lay him down on his left side or have him stand with his right side facing you. Starting on the back hip, begin what is called *line brushing*. Vertically part the hair from the buttocks to right in front of the rear leg. Take this section and layer it horizontally about an inch at a time, starting with the lower hair on the leg and working up toward the part on the back. With each layer, spray a little antistatic mist or conditioning mist on the hair and brush gently, bringing the brush all the way past the ends of the hair. Never brush the hair dry because this causes

breakage. Always hold the brush by the handle and take care not to flip the brush upward at the end of the stroke; this can be damaging to the ends of the hair. Repeat this process with each section, working towards the head. Part, lightly mist and brush.

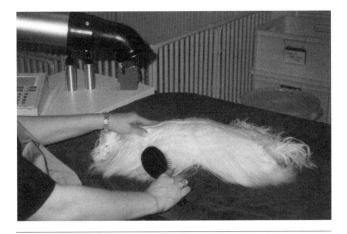

Part the hair in sections and lightly mist before you brush gently. (Photo by Larry Abbott)

Should you find any mats while brushing, use your fingers to pull the mat apart gently and your comb to work it out, losing the least amount of hair possible. Do not cut or pull out the matted hair. Applying coat conditioner to the mat can sometimes help pry it apart. Turn the dog over or around to the left side and do the same procedure on that side. After the left side is finished, stand the puppy up if he is lying down, brush the hair under the tail in sections and brush the hair on the tail. Now it is time to do the chest. Brush the chest hair in layers as well.

Brush and comb the hair on the top of your puppy's head as well as his ear hair. After brushing the ear hair, run a comb gently through the same area. The tip of the ear leather can be split very easily because it is very thin, so always be aware of where the skin is on the ear when you are getting mats out of this area. Mats will very often develop behind the ears, so make sure you have brushed this area. Use your fine-toothed comb around the face, being very careful not to catch the eye rim or to poke the eye. If your puppy has some eye stain, use a soft makeup brush with a long handle to apply cornstarch to the hair. Rub in the cornstarch, press it into the hair with a dry cloth and then comb through the hair with your fine-toothed comb. This will help lighten the stain over a period of time. Do not use baby powder for this because it gets gummy in the hair when the tears make it wet. Cornstarch will absorb the moisture better.

Now you are all through grooming except for the topknot. On a puppy, you are lucky if whatever you put in the hair stays in for more than a few minutes after you let him go; but as the puppy matures, if you have been consistent about putting his topknot back up, he will gradually get used to it being there. For very young dogs, it is easier just to start with a small latex rubber band made for this purpose. Orthodontic rubber bands will work as well. Part the hair with the steel end of the ratting comb. Make the part from the corner of the eye back to right in front of the ear on both sides of the head. Then part from one ear to the other on the head in front of the ears. Pull this section of hair up above the head and put it into the

rubber band. Take care that your dog's eyes are not pulled tight. If you need to loosen the hair at the eye, pull the hair above the eye toward you a little.

To start out with, your puppy's hair can be pulled up in a rubber band with the hair sticking out of the top making a fountain-like effect. When he learns to leave this up, you can start doing topknots with bows. (Photo by Larry Abbott)

When your Maltese is a little older and is used to the rubber bands, you can put up two topknots and even add bows!

Many Maltese owners prefer to keep their dogs clipped short in what is called a *puppy trim*. This is a cute trim, and it will keep a Maltese of any age looking like a puppy. This trim can be done by a professional groomer, or you can ask your breeder how to do it on your own. With this trim, the whiskers, ears, tail and sometimes head hair are left fairly long while the rest of the body is trimmed to the length the owner desires. We recommend this for anyone who still wants the look of the Maltese but not necessarily all the work of a very long coat. It is very comfortable for the dog and causes less pain in the long run because it mats less.

Finding a Groomer

Not all groomers can do a Maltese. For some reason, they want to trim hair around the eyes and make them look like Poodles. To find a groomer who knows something about what you want your Maltese to look like, ask your breeder for a

You can trim your Maltese in a puppy cut or in a special trim like this. Either trim is very comfortable for the dog and less work for you! (Photo by M. Martin)

recommendation. If the breeder is not in your area, try asking your veterinarian or contact other Maltese owners or breeders. As a last resort, try having your dog groomed at a well-respected grooming establishment near you. Let them know exactly what you expect your dog to look like when you pick him up. Also check out how they treat their canine customers. Avoid grooming places that want to tranquilize your dog to groom him.

GROWING AND CARING FOR THE MALTESE SHOW COAT
Selective Breeding

Before you look at taking care of the Maltese coat for show, let's look at the coat you have to take care of. Does the puppy you selected come from breeding that has full, fast-growing coats? Or do they have slow-growing coats? Is the hair shiny and white or dull and brittle? If the puppy's slow coat growth is hereditary, products may condition but will probably not make the coat grow faster. There is also a possibility that disease or certain conditions can be hereditary. These can affect coat growth and can cause internal deficiencies that compromise coat quality and condition. It *is* possible to repair and condition coats caused by these things, but it is good to rule them out as a cause of the coat problem before proceeding with months of conditioning.

Internal things can affect hair growth:

1. Too little thyroid hormone—impairs hair growth (hypothyroidism)

2. Too much female hormone—slows hair growth (excess estrogen)

3. Hormone imbalance—coat too thin, brittle

4. Parasites—produce dry, brittle coat

5. Vitamin deficiency—produces dry, brittle coat

6. Fat-intake deficiency—produces dull, dry coat

7. Pregnancy—can cause stress resulting in hair loss

8. Cortisone excess (adrenal gland hyperfunction)—can happen if the dog is on steroids for a long time; causes hair loss or damage

9. Estrogen deficiency—causes scanty hair growth

10. Demodectic mange—sometimes brought on by stress, causes hair loss

11. Allergy to food or pollens—can cause severe rashes or itching and scratching resulting in hair loss

Scrapper's breeding gave him the genes to produce this glorious coat. (He had a little help with the grooming from Vicki.) (Photo by Vicki Abbott)

If you think your dog's coat shows these symptoms no matter what you do to care for it, you should plan a visit to the veterinarian to rule out any internal possibilities for the coat damage.

Nutrition for Coat Care

Nutrition is extremely important for a healthy coat. An adequate amount of fat is a necessity in a dog's diet for the production of natural oils. Natural oils lubricate the skin's surface. These oils help retain heat and prevent evaporation, thereby moisturizing the skin. They also lubricate the hair shaft itself. Make sure your potential show dog has the best and most natural food available without all the chemical preservatives or additives such as Ethoxyquin, BHA or BHT. Supplement his diet with good vitamins and enzymes for optimum health. If he is healthy on the inside, the results will show on the outside in a luxurious, shiny coat.

Climate and Water Type

Climate and type of water have an effect on the Maltese coat. Dry climates can cause static and breakage to the coat. Humid climates cause more matting and clumping and cause the brush to drag through the hair.

The water you bathe your dog in is different depending on the location in which you live. Shampoo has a sudsing action in soft water and can be harder to get rinsed completely out of the coat. Hard water produces fewer suds and rinses easier, but it can also leave trace mineral deposits on the hair that will build up over a period of time. Chlorine found in tap water can be devastating to the Maltese coat. The chlorine breaks down the hair protein and accelerates oxidation.

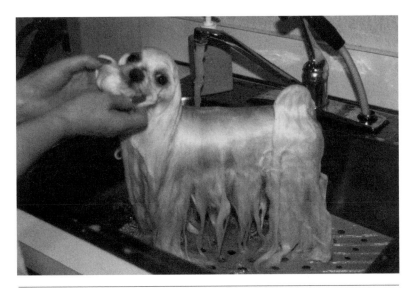

The water you bathe your Maltese in can have a lot to do with the condition of his coat over a period of time. (Photo by Vicki Abbott)

Oxidation causes hair to become dry and appear dull. Sodium bisulfate can be found in some shampoos to offset the bonding action of chlorine.

Hair Care Products for the Maltese Coat

Proper care and treatment of hair requires good hair products. Certain products can remove excess amounts of natural oils and moisture from the hair, making it dry and brittle. Then hair conditioners are necessary to restore the oils. Choose hair products based on safety, whether they are designed and tested for the Maltese and whether they have a history of working on this type of coat.

Hair grows in cycles—periods of growth and periods of rest. All individual hair follicles may be in different phases. Two key words for those in a hurry are *patience* and *perseverance*! Keeping the coat and skin in good condition on your Maltese at all times is not optional if you wish to show him. From the time your puppy has his first bath, good-quality hair care products should be used.

Shampoos

You might need a shampoo to:

1. Brighten whites without leaving your dog blue or gray (porous hair will absorb color)

2. Put protein in the hair shaft by penetrating and absorbing

3. Help heal troubled skin

4. Moisturize

5. Be tearless and nonirritating to the eyes

6. Be hypoallergenic if you have a dog that is sensitive

7. Add body to the coat

8. Improve the manageability of the coat

9. Help eliminate urine stains on feet

10. Remove conditioning oil

11. Contain no dyes that can stain the hair

Obviously, you must decide what your needs are for your dog's particular coat. Every Maltese is different, and since we all live in a different place where the water plays a big part in the results, you will need to try a good shampoo or two before you can decide which one works the best for you. Avoid shampoos that contain alcohol because this is very drying.

Ask the breeder of your show puppy what he suggests and what he used on the puppy before you acquired him. He should be willing to help you out with suggestions, especially since it's his puppy you are planning to show!

Conditioners

You might need a hair conditioner to:

1. Strengthen the hair shaft

2. Provide antistatic to the hair

3. Detangle

4. Coat the hair shaft for protection from the elements

5. Penetrate the hair shaft for moisture absorption

6. Leave no residue

Conditioners are designed to restore the hair shaft to its natural condition. Some conditioners can tend to make the Maltese hair too soft and fly-away. Again, this is a trial-and-error process to find what works the best on your dog's coat. It may be necessary at times to deep condition the coat, leaving the conditioner on the coat after it has been shampooed and wrapping the dog in a warm towel for a while before rinsing. This will allow the conditioner to penetrate into the cuticle and produce better healing results.

Finishing Sprays and Creams

You might want a finishing spray or cream to:

1. Promote shine

2. Provide antistatic

3. Provide manageability in the show ring

4. Reduce hair breakage while brushing

5. Care for damaged hair, especially on the ends

6. Condition

7. Be used as a light mist for brushing between shows

There have been many advances in the last few years regarding products to use on the day of the show. The main purpose of these products is to produce a manageable and static-free Maltese coat in the show ring after you have spent all that time grooming. The product you use must not be detectable in the coat as the dog is being examined. Static can often be a problem in dry areas of the country or at certain times of the year. This will make the coat look fly-away and can cause breakage. A finishing spray or a light cream will make the coat lay down and produce a more "finished" look.

Oiling Your Show Dog

Your show dog should be bathed every seven to ten days from the time he is just an 8-week-old puppy. Until he is about 6 months old, a regular bath using a good shampoo and conditioner, as well as daily brushing, should be plenty to keep his coat in good shape. Always mist the coat with a good conditioning mist or antistatic spray while brushing. Wrap the topknot hair and whiskers as soon as length permits.

When the coat starts to get longer, you may want to put it in oil or wrap it. The age at which you start this will be somewhere between 6 and 12 months old. When the coat reaches floor length, you should start wrapping the body hair. Oil is a natural humectant. Some coats need it; others do not. Some climates cause coats to mat more frequently, and oil helps keep hair separated. Also, oil treats split ends and protects hair from sun, wind and damage. Dirt lays on top of the oil and cannot penetrate to the hair shaft itself.

If a dog is in oil and wraps, you *must* brush and rewrap him on a daily basis. Check the coat often

to make sure it is not gumming up. If the entire coat is not saturated with the oil, you can get dry and oily spots that will tend to fuse together into a mat.

This little girl is in oil getting ready for her show career. (Photo by Larry Abbott)

Sometimes the dog's sebaceous glands do not produce enough oil to get to the ends of the hair shaft. A dog in oil will have the entire hair shaft lubricated. Oil helps prevent moisture from evaporating. Oiled coats can sometimes look yellowish in color, but this color will rinse out. Always use a water-soluble, or emulsifying, oil. You can tell if it meets this requirement by putting a drop in water—if it clouds up, it is water soluble. If it beads up, it is not. A water-soluble oil will coat and penetrate the hair shaft to condition it.

To put a Maltese in oil, put about two tablespoons to one-fourth cup of oil per two quarts of warm water in a pitcher. The amount of oil you use will depend on the texture and density of the coat. The more dense the coat, the more oil you add to the pitcher. It really does not take much. After you have shampooed and conditioned the coat, and while the dog is still in the sink, pour the oil over the dog, working it into the coat. Do not rinse the oil out; just squeeze out the excess in the sink. Dry the dog with your stand dryer. (If you feel the coat needs a little extra conditioning, you can add a teaspoon or so of conditioner to the oil before you pour it over the dog.)

When the coat starts to reach the floor, you may need to wrap all or part of the hair up to keep it from damage. Ch. Scylla's Don't Take Me Litely is in oil and partially wrapped for conditioning. (Photo by Larry & Vicki Abbott)

Some dogs only need a light spray oil; others need to be rinsed with it and blow dried. The name of the game with all products is to be creative to find out what works for you. If the shampoo you like makes your dog's coat too soft in your water, dilute it and see if that makes a difference. Hit your niche with your particular dog. If

you stay within one product line that you find to be dependable, you will get the best results. Some shampoos and conditioners have been researched and produced to work together. Follow the manufacturer's suggestions and call them if you have a question.

Wrapping Your Maltese

When you wrap, you must decide how many sections you will part the hair into and how many wrappers you will use. The smaller and tighter the sections, the more the hair will tend to fuse together at the rubber band. There are wrappers made specifically for show dogs that you can order, or you can purchase the type of waxed paper sheets used in picking up donuts. All of these sheets are precut and are the right size for wrapping a section of Maltese hair. Section the hair and lightly mist the section before you brush through it. Use a spray bottle containing a little of the same oil already in the coat mixed with distilled water. Fold the wrapper over a little at the top and place it under the section of hair. Trifold the paper around the section of hair and fold it up towards the dog two to three times, depending on the length of the hair and the wrapper. Place a rubber band around the middle of the wrapper. Be careful when you wrap the ears and tail not to get any part of the ear leather or the actual tail in the rubber banded part of the wrapper; this can cut off the blood supply and can cause damage to these parts of the body.

When wrapping whiskers, make sure that only the hair from the top of the dog's mouth is included in the wrap—don't wrap your dog's mouth shut by getting chin hair in with hair from the top of the mouth! Spraying a product such as Bitter Apple on the wrappers can keep your dog from attempting to chew on the wrappers or the rubber bands.

Scylla's Nothin' But Net, known as Dunk'n, finds that being in wrappers doesn't inhibit the fun times he enjoys with Larry . (Photo by Larry & Vicki Abbott)

PREPARING THE MALTESE FOR SHOW DAY

You have bathed, dried, wrapped, unwrapped, brushed and combed your Maltese puppy's coat for the purpose of presenting a beautifully conditioned dog in the ring on the day of the dog show. The show is on Saturday. What do you do now?

Trim the Nails and Toe Pad Hair

Make sure your dog's nails are trimmed a couple of days before the show. Do this so that, in case you happen to hit the quick on a nail, your dog will be fine by the show day. If you neglect to remember this tip, the best-groomed dog could possibly limp or hop and be excused from the ring because of a tender toenail! The same goes for hair between the toe pads. Very carefully trim the hair so the judge can see each black toe pad if necessary. Should you nick a nail or toe pad, apply Kwik Stop to stop the bleeding. Doing nails and toe pads ahead of time also allows for bathing out anything that gets into the coat during this procedure.

Teeth

It might be wise to pay attention to making sure your dog's teeth are clean a few days before the show. Judges like looking into mouths with white sparkly teeth rather than mouths with yellow teeth and bad odor. Many products are available to help you keep your dog's teeth clean—scalars, teeth-cleaning pads, dog toothpaste and toothbrushes and so on—so there is no excuse for a dirty mouth.

This is just good practice for the rest of your dog's life.

When to Bathe Your Dog

Decide whether you will bathe your dog the day before or the morning of the show. I would estimate two or three hours to bathe, dry and groom your dog for the ring. There are three things to consider here—the time you have available, the kind of coat you are dealing with and the stamina or attitude of your dog. If your ring time is late afternoon, you may have time to bathe your dog on the day of the show.

If your ring time is at 8A.M., however, do the bathing the day before. Always overestimate the time you will need. If your dog has an abundance of coat, a night's rest after it has been washed may make the coat lay better, especially after natural oils

Make sure all tangles are out of the coat before wetting it down for a bath. (Photo by Larry Abbott)

have been brushed back into it. If you have a dog with a thinner coat, it could look oily by the next day. You will have to determine this before the actual show weekend. Another thing to consider is your dog's attitude. If you bathe and groom the morning of the show, will your dog be so tired or irritated with you that he will not show well? Or, on the other hand, does he have a personality that could use a little calming down on show day?

Tricks to Bathing and Drying

The shampoo and conditioner you use will play a big role in how the coat will look and handle after it is dried. The pH balance for products you need for your Maltese coat is around level five. Products for human hair can be higher—seven or above. Higher pH levels can damage or dry out hair, so be careful when using human products.

Brush your dog's coat to make sure there is no matting of the hair before it is washed. This is a *very* important step that you cannot skip, or you will end up with a wad you will never be able to pry apart. For your first shampooing, apply a shampoo that will cut through and rinse out any oil or dirt currently in the coat. Work it into the coat carefully without swirling or tangling the hair. Then rinse well. Shampoo again, applying either the same shampoo or one that moisturizes, conditions or whitens, depending on the needs of the coat. Rinse well again. Apply a conditioner of your choice and leave it in for a few minutes. Then rinse and squeeze the excess water gently out of the dog's hair like you would a fine sweater. Wrap the dog in a towel and head for the dryer. The longer you let the coat air dry without using a dryer, the less straight it will end up.

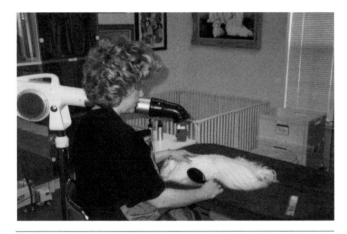

Using a large stand dryer will free up both of your hands to deal with the hair while you are brushing. You need a dryer that has enough force to dry the coat effectively, not one that will blow the dog off the table! (Photo by Larry Abbott)

There are two ways to blow dry your dog:

1. *The first way:* Turn the dog tummy up in your lap. Dry the feet, the tummy hair and the underneath part of the chest hair and back skirts. Then stand or lay the dog on the table. Dry the show side (left side) first and then the nonshow side, moving to the rear. Finally, dry the chest, head hair and ears. Keep some distilled water in a spray bottle so that, if any part of the hair does not dry straight, you can mist it and dry it again. Do not try to part hair while it is wet because it will break. The part should be made before he is bathed.

2. *The second way:* Stand or lay the dog on a table and blow dry the show-side hair first. Move to the nonshow side and the rear. Dry the chest, head hair and ears. Finally, dry the feet and tummy hair.

Whichever way you choose to accomplish drying your Maltese is a matter of preference and what tends to dry out first on your particular dog. When he is dry (make sure the ears are *thoroughly* dry because they take the longest), put up the head hair in a topknot and the facial hair in whisker wraps. If the hair seems really fluffy or soft, you may want to brush an antistatic spray or cream into the coat before you put the dog to bed for the night.

Trimming the Feet

Maltese can have the appearance of wearing giant bedroom slippers, or movement may look wrong when it actually is not, due to improperly trimmed or untrimmed feet. There is really not a lot of trimming to do—just rounding or straightening up the scraggly appearance to make it look neater. This should be done immediately after drying and wrapping. Side hair should be wrapped up temporarily so you do not trim that hair accidentally along with the hair on the feet. The length of your dog's coat may be trimmed even to the floor to facilitate movement. Move your Maltese after trimming to make sure he is not tripping on hair. Trimming hair length should be done with the dog standing in a natural position.

Final Touches

Now your Maltese is ready for the final grooming touches: ironing the coat and putting up topknots.

Ironing the Coat

If you plan to use a hair straightener or a hair iron, you will need to purchase one at your local beauty-supply store. Choose from the ones that have controllable heat so you do not damage your dog's hair.

On the day of the show, start by laying the dog in your lap. Comb through the hair on the feet and brush all the tummy hair.

Turn the dog over to stand or lay on the table. Make a straight part down the dog's back from between the ears to the root of the tail. Starting

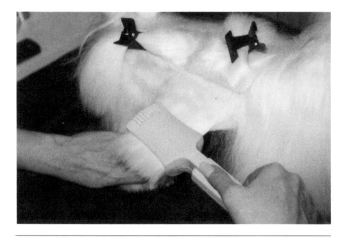

Iron the coat in sections by starting an inch away from the part and ironing past the ends of the hair to lessen the possibility of damage. (Photo by Larry Abbott)

with the nonshow side at the neck and using 2- to 3-inch sections at a time, layer the hair and brush—always downward. After brushing each layer, you have the *option* to iron and/or apply antistatic spray or cream to that layer of coat. By the time you have brushed the top section, the coat should lay pretty nicely. (No amount of product or ironing is going to make a cottony, wooly or curly coat correct, but there are many fairly nice coats that will look 100% better if the right techniques and products are used on them.) Continue around to the back, the show side and then the chest and head. Now you are ready for the topknots.

Topknots

The key to doing good topknots is to keep in mind that each dog's head you will be dealing with is different, so you cannot do topknots the same on every dog. Make a picture in your mind of where those bows need to end up to create and maintain a balanced look to the head. Try not to make huge topknots and bows on a dog with smaller eyes and nose. Conversely, do not put teeny topknots and bows on a dog with nice big eyes and same size nose. Consider the color of your bows. Maybe your favorite color is red, but does that color enhance or take away from the dark points on your Maltese? A Maltese face should be enhanced by the topknots and bows. Therefore, you must be able to *see* his face and not watch them bouncing off his nose with every move.

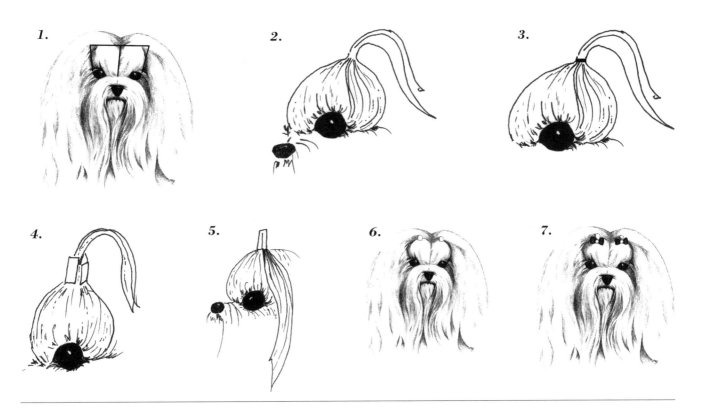

1. *Brush the head hair back over the skull between the ears. Make a part up the middle of the head from the nose between the eyes to a point between the ears. Where that point is will be determined largely by the shape of the dog's head and the placement of the ears. Now make a part from the outer corner of each eye upward toward the ear. You will end up with two sections of hair, one above each eye, shaped slightly like a triangle. (Illustration by Kathy Blackard)* **2.** *Start with the right side. To backcomb the hair and have it stay, divide the triangle into three sections. Backcomb each section individually. Then put them all together, smoothing the hair on the outside with your ratting comb. (Illustration by Judy Lambert)* **3.** *Put a little rubber band, twisted twice, on this section of topknot hair. Do the other side the same way. (Illustration by Judy Lambert)* **4.** *Now you can move and position the topknots so they are balanced on the head, or you can take one or both down and try again. When they are positioned how you want them, wrap a little piece of tissue paper or netting around the hair at the rubber band. (Illustration by Judy Lambert)* **5.** *Fold it over towards the back of the head. (Illustration by Judy Lambert)* **6.** *Put another little rubber band over the paper to hold it in place. Repeat steps 4 and 5 on the other side. (Illustration by Kathy Blackard)* **7.** *Add bows with either rubber bands or twist ties attached to them to hold them in place. (Illustration by Kathy Blackard)*

Last Minute Hints

Believe it or not, putting a lead on a groomed dog can be a trick. Lift the hair you want above the lead before putting it on. Then lower the hair over the lead after it is in place. This makes for a smoother look and does not allow the hair to catch in the lead as badly.

A good antistatic spray or cream in a pocket-size bottle can be helpful in controlling the coat outside the ring. Be sure to spray far enough away from the coat and allow enough time for it to dry before examination by the judge.

Use of a little cornstarch in the whiskers can whiten them up before ring time—just make sure you get it all out before entering the ring.

Some people use bait, or treats, to get the dog's attention in the ring. As long as it is held in your hand and not thrown everywhere in the ring, this is fine. Squeaky toys can also be used as attention-getters, but use them sparingly to avoid a frown from the judge or fellow exhibitors.

Frank Oberstar puts the finishing touches on one of his Maltese before going into the ring. (Photo by Frank Oberstar & Larry Ward)

After the Show

When the showing is done, it is best to put the dog back into wrappers as soon as possible to avoid hair being chewed or becoming urine stained. Brush through the coat carefully, applying antistatic spray or conditioning cream. Wrap the head, whiskers and ear hair. Depending on the length of the coat, also wrap up the rear skirts and tail hair. This will keep the hair from damage until you can get home.

Do not leave the dog this way for days, especially if he was in oil before the show. As soon as possible, brush, bathe and put your dog back in oil and wraps. If you are not using oil, just brush, bathe and condition. This removes any damaging grooming products or dirt from the hair that accumulated in the coat at the show.

Above all, you should make this entire grooming process a pleasant one for both you and your dog. Don't lose patience with your Maltese

With all the final touches completed, Henry waits his turn to go into the ring. (Photo by Larry Abbott)

because you were tired before you started grooming or didn't allow yourself enough time. If the dog considers grooming and showing to be a happy time—a time when he gets undivided attention from you—you will have a happy dog on the end of your lead.

(Photo by Michelle Perlmutter)

CHAPTER NINE

Showing Your Maltese

T he sport of purebred dogs can be exciting and frustrating at the same time. Before you attempt to get heavily involved in the idea of showing your dog, it would be wise to become more familiar with what this would involve. Understanding the dog world before you plunge into it can save you a lot of headaches. Seek help from an appropriate source. Talk to the breeder of your dog or puppy to find out where to go for information and attend local dog shows to watch and get an idea of the basics.

THE HISTORY OF THE SPORT

The sport of showing dogs has been popular for a very long time. The Kennel Club in England was formed in 1859, the American Kennel Club was established in 1884 and the Canadian Kennel Club was formed in 1888. The purpose of these clubs was to form a registry of purebred dogs and maintain their stud books. More than 36 million dogs have been enrolled in the AKC stud book since 1888. The first Maltese to be registered in the United States was a dog named Topsy, in 1888.

Today, the kennel clubs register dogs and adopt and enforce rules and regulations governing dog shows, obedience trials and field trials. There are many activities that exist for the enjoyment of both the dog and the owner. Some of the activities include conformation showing, obedience competition, tracking, agility and the Canine Good Citizen Certificate. Where you start really depends on your goals. This sport is taken very seriously by some as a profession and by others as only a hobby. Whatever the case may be for you, realize that, once you start, you may be hooked for life!

The Maltese judging at the Beverly Hills Kennel Club. Henry, left, with Vicki, went on to win the Breed and Group First. (Photo by Larry Abbott)

Conformation Showing

When you exhibit your dog in the conformation ring, he will be judged on how closely he adheres to the standard for Maltese. This is based on the dog's appearance, movement and attitude. If you are considering this type of showing, be aware of how to evaluate your dog compared to the standard. This will take some instruction from a knowledgeable person willing to help you. Experienced breeders are familiar with selecting puppies from a litter based on their qualities. Unfortunately, puppies sometimes can go through lots of changes as they mature, which can get very frustrating. If a puppy starts out as a very hopeful candidate for the show ring, he may go through several stages where he looks good, bad and then good again. That is why some breeders will hold onto their promising puppies until they reach the age where they are probably not going to change any more.

Conformation classes are sometimes offered by the local kennel club, obedience club or a dog handler in the area. Your puppy will need to know how to walk on a lead before you decide to show him. At the classes, you can learn proper ring procedure and techniques for posing (or stacking) and gaiting your puppy. When the judge instructs you to move your dog in the ring, he can decide to use different patterns for you to move in such as the "triangle" or the "L." These classes can give you confidence, and you will know what you are doing when your walk into that ring. A conformation class is also a good way for your puppy to be socialized to other dogs and different people so that, when he is at a show, it will seem normal to him.

Conformation matches are sometimes offered by kennel clubs in conjunction with their all-breed show. They may be AKC sanctioned matches or just fun matches. A puppy can usually be entered in these matches from the time he is 3 months old until he's a year old. There may even be classes offered for adults. Both you and your puppy can gain confidence from attending a match. You will get an idea of how your puppy is going to act on the end of a lead in these surroundings, and you will know what you need to work on. These matches are usually conducted similarly to point shows, where the classes are divided by age, and the winners of those classes compete for Best of Breed or Variety. The winner of the Breed goes on to compete in the Group, and the winner of the Group goes on to compete for Best in Match.

Although no championship points are awarded at these matches, some exhibitors take them very seriously, and the experience your puppy will get can be very valuable in the conformation ring later on. At the match, it is great for your puppy to be touched by new people and be exposed to new noises and smells.

To earn a championship, a dog must accumulate the appropriate number of points. To become an AKC Champion of Record, the dog must earn fifteen points. The number of points earned each time the dog is shown depends on the number of dogs in competition. The United States is divided into twelve zones. Each zone has its own set of points. The number of points available at each show depends on the breed, its sex and the location of the show. The purpose of the zones is to try to equalize the points available from breed to breed and area to area. The American Kennel Club adjusts the point system on a yearly basis in the spring. It is good for you to know how many dogs or bitches it takes to achieve a certain number of points for your area.

The maximum amount of points your dog can win at one show is five. When the dog wins three, four or five points at one time, these wins are

Velvet, a Crisandra puppy, is just 4 months old and is doing very well at the match! (Photo by Sandra Kenner & Christine Pearson)

called majors. Your dog will need fifteen points won under at least three different judges including two majors won under different judges. Canada works on a point system as well, but majors are not required.

There are a variety of classes in which you can enter your dog. If your dog is under a year of age, he can be entered in a puppy class. Sometimes these puppy classes are divided by age—6 to 9 months old and 9 to 12 months old. There is a 12- to 18-month-old class, a Novice class, a

Bred-by-Exhibitor class, an American-bred class and an Open class.

Vicki's daughter Tara exhibits one of their class Maltese, who won Winners Dog, Best of Winners and Best of Breed on the same day. (Photo by Pegini Animal Photo)

Dogs of the same sex compete against each other to begin with. Males (dogs) compete before bitches. The class winners of the same sex of each breed or variety compete against each other for Winners Dog and Winners Bitch. A Reserve Winners Dog and Reserve Winners Bitch are also selected by the judge, but this award does not carry any points unless the Winners award is disallowed by AKC for some reason. The Winners Dog and Winners Bitch compete with the specials (champions) for Best of Breed or Variety, Best of Winners and Best of Opposite Sex.

It is possible for your dog to pick up an extra point or even a major if the points were higher for the dog that your Maltese defeated or if he defeats a champion.

If you are at an all-breed show, the Best of Breed winners for each Toy breed will go on to the Toy Group. This is true for each respective group. There are seven groups: Sporting, Hound, Working, Terriers, Toys, Non-Sporting, and Herding. The winners of the Groups then go on to compete for Best in Show.

A Specialty show is a show in which only one breed is exhibited. There are a few Specialty shows held by Maltese clubs in different parts of the country. The American Maltese Association holds one national Maltese specialty per year on a rotating basis between the East, West and Midwest areas of the United States. At a Specialty show, the highest award competed for is Best of Breed, and there are no Group or Best in Show competitions. The AMA also holds a Puppy Sweepstakes in conjunction with the National. No points are awarded in this competition, but breeders exhibit their puppies for the prestigious Best in Sweepstakes award.

In the United States, a dog may receive the award for Dual or Triple Champion. The Dual Champion must be a Champion of Record and either a Champion Tracker, a Herding Champion, an Obedience Trial Champion or a Field Champion. Any dog that has been awarded the titles of Champion of Record and any two of the following—Champion Tracker, Herding Champion, Obedience Trial Champion or Field Champion—may be designated as a Triple Champion.

Debra Kirsch is shown with her puppy that won the AMA Sweepstakes under breeder-judge Vicki Abbott at the National Specialty in 1988. (Photo by Missy Yuhl)

THE OLDEST KENNEL CLUB SHOW

Although there are many prestigious kennel club shows in the United States, Westminster Kennel Club is the oldest. The entry is limited to 2,500 dogs, and it is held at Madison Square Garden in New York. Many years ago, this show allowed for entries in all classes; today, however, only champions can be entered.

At a show such as this, the quality of the dogs is usually superb. It is a good show to watch to become familiar with the different breeds. The show is televised as are many other dog shows today. It is also one of the few shows in this country that is still benched. In past history of this sport in the United States, many dog shows were benched. A "benched" show is one in which the dog must be on a bench during the show except when actually in the ring. This allows spectators to view the animals and can be a great learning experience.

THE LARGEST DOG SHOW IN THE WORLD

Crufts, the largest dog show in the world, is held by The Kennel Club in England. It has been reported that they have had entries numbering close to 20,000 dogs. The show lasts four days. Entry is gained through qualifying by winning classes at other championship shows. Crufts exhibitors can show their dogs in conformation, obedience or agility.

Westminster Kennel Club in the early 1990s—Vicki Abbott showing Champion Sand Island Small Kraft Lite in the Group. (Photo by Michelle Perlmutter)

Earning a championship in England differs from the United States in that they do not have a point system. Challenge Certificates are awarded if the judge feels the dog is deserving regardless of the number of dogs in competition. A dog must earn three Challenge Certificates under three different judges with at least one of the Certificates being won after the age of 12 months. The shows in England seem to put more emphasis on breeder judges than the shows in the United States. There is quite a bit of competition in the individual breeds, which keeps the quality high. In the United States, more emphasis is put on the Group and Best in Show wins, and they are promoted accordingly. There are more multiple-breed judges at the all-breed shows, and breeder judges tend to be used more at the specialty shows. The shows in England can be very large and extend over several days. Usually shows in the United States last for one day at a time for each kennel club, although different kennel clubs can "cluster" together to make what is called a "circuit" of two, three or many days of shows at a time.

TRAVELING WITH YOUR MALTESE

We insert this section here because it is inevitable that you will travel with your Maltese if your plans are to show him. But these tips and guidelines can be applied to any travel with your pet. A Maltese is just the right size to take with you anywhere. He will enjoy being in your company and really does not require too much in the way of extra care on a trip. Following some guidelines can ensure the safety of your dog while traveling.

Travel by Car

The earlier you start getting your puppy used to travel the better. Some dogs are nervous when they travel and may get carsick. This can be a problem if you have already bathed your dog for the show before traveling. Although there are medications your veterinarian can give you for this, it is better to start the puppy out on short trips; more than likely, he will get used to the motion of the car by the time you need to show him. Do not always make the trips to the veterinarian for a shot. Your Maltese needs to feel that going for a ride is a fun thing!

Let your puppy out to relieve himself before you travel. Be prepared for a possible accident and cleanup by bringing towels or tissues with you. If you have already bathed your dog for the show and he happens to get sick on the way, you can use a spray bottle containing some distilled water to clean him up a bit, and you can squeeze his hair in a hand towel to get the water out.

Your dog or puppy needs to be kept in a safe place while traveling. The best idea is to put him in a fiberglass crate that he is used to going in and out of at home. If you are not worried about keeping his hair in place and are just going for a ride, you can also use a harness made for dogs. Obviously, a Maltese or any dog should not ride in the back of a pickup truck. Besides getting all kinds of foreign objects in their eyes, dogs can be

Your Maltese can travel safely in the car in their own separate crates. (Photo by Larry Abbott)

nearby highway. The owners didn't even know he was gone until hours later and miles away! He had been injured and was scratching at the door for help. Don't lose your dog this way—you may never find him.

Leaving a dog loose in a car with a collar and leash on can also be disastrous. This can result in the dog hanging himself. And last, but of *ultimate* importance—*never leave your dog unattended in a car.* Even rolling the windows down usually is not enough when the temperature inside the car could soar to over 100°F. Your Maltese also could get stolen. You might think you are only going to be gone for a minute, but you may be sorry when you get back.

Where to Stay

Many motels and hotels do allow dogs, even some very first-class ones. Call ahead to motels or hotels before you travel to see if they will accept your small pet. Some places will accept small dogs but not large ones. It may also be necessary to put down a deposit against any room damage. There are several books that provide listings of pet-friendly accommodations nationwide.

thrown from the truck and be injured or killed. I'll never forget the time we thought a burglar was breaking into our home one evening, only to discovered it was a Labrador Retriever that had bounced out of the back of a pickup truck on the

If you leave your room while staying at your hotel, make sure your dog is safe in his crate. If your dog happens to be a barker, it would be a wise idea to turn on the television. This will help deaden the noises he may make. Do your share in keeping the room clean during your stay so that others may have the same privilege in the future

If you live in the North, you could possibly drive to Canada to show your dogs as well as showing them in the United States. Here, Elsie Burke (right) wins Best of Breed with American Canadian Champion Scylla's Wonder's Mayan Pawper and wins the Puppy Group with Louan's Apache Starfire. (Photo by Alex Smith)

of having their dogs with them. This applies to the outside of the hotel or motel premises as well, where you may exercise your dog.

Travel by Air

If you decide to go to a show by air or are traveling with your Maltese on a plane for vacation, you will need to contact the airlines to check their policies regarding pets. Many major airlines will allow you to put your Maltese under the seat in front of you in an appropriate carrier. This requires a reservation for the dog and payment in advance. You can purchase your carrying case at a pet store

or through the airlines. A good case for a Maltese is the Sherpa Bag, which is designed specifically for this purpose and comes in a variety of sizes and colors. The Kennel Cab II also is a good carrier if you prefer one that is hard-sided. The case must not be taller than 12 or 13 inches high to fit under the airline seat.

There should always be adequate ventilation for your dog in any carrying case you choose.

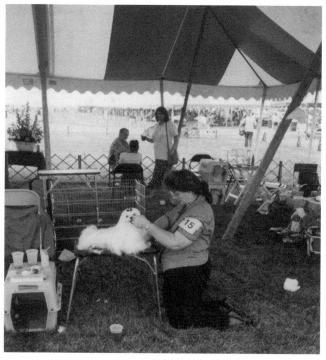

Barbara Cantlon grooms Ch. Marcris Risque Omen on the weekend he won the National Specialty in 1998. Barbara was one of many exhibitors who traveled by air with their dogs to attend the Specialty. Omen is bred and owned by Joyce Watkins. (Photo by Vicki Abbott)

Allow your dog to get accustomed to this new type of carrier before the day you need to use it.

It is preferable to schedule a direct flight when traveling with your Maltese, keeping the time he has to stay in the crate at a minimum. Commuter planes are usually not a good choice for travel with your pet because they can be cramped and loud. Some commuter planes do not even allow pets on board. The Humane Society of the United States has put together a tip sheet for airline traveling with your pet. You can obtain a copy by sending a self-addressed, stamped envelope to: The Humane Society of the United States, Tip Sheet, 2100 L Street NW, Washington DC 20037. Regulations for travel out of the country are different and are sometimes changed without notice. Give yourself plenty of lead time to contact the appropriate consulate or agricultural department for instructions. Some countries have very lengthy quarantines. These can extend up to six months. (This is definitely when your little Maltese should stay at home with a friend.) Countries may differ in their inoculations required and may possibly request that they be given at a certain time before the dog enters the country. For instance, a rabies vaccine may be required no less than thirty days before the trip.

Identification

When you travel, make sure your dog is wearing proper identification. If there is an accident and the dog gets loose or he just happens to escape and run away, your name and phone number need to be on the dog somewhere. Collars with engraved nameplates are a good idea; however, collars on a show dog can tear hair. They also can get separated from your pet, or the tags can fall off. Owners have been tattooing their dogs for several years for identification purposes.

If you wish to tattoo your dog, use your social security number so the humane shelters will have a way to trace it. Tattoos with just a registry number can be a problem because there are several registries to check. The tattoo is usually done on the inside of the right thigh. You may need to use a collar and tags for awhile before you tattoo; the thigh area on your Maltese may be too small when he is a puppy, and the tattoo will tend to be stretched with growth. Contact your veterinarian if you wish to tattoo your dog.

The newest method of identification is microchipping. This little microchip is no larger than a grain of rice. Your veterinarian will implant the chip between the shoulder blades of your dog. The dog should feel no discomfort with the chip in place. Each chip has its own code and can be identified by using a scanner. A dog's owner can be easily traced by the humane society or by anyone who has a microchip scanner, and the scanner will work on any brand of microchip. There are several registries in the United States for microchip identification.

WHEN YOU ARE AWAY

There may be a time when you will need to travel without your Maltese. The ideal place for your dog would obviously be in his own home if you have to leave him.

If at all possible, when you must travel without your Maltese, it is always best to leave him in his own home with someone you can trust to care for him. (Photo by Julie Phillips)

There are people who will come to your home to take care of your dog if you cannot find a friend or relative willing to do this. They may also be willing to care for the dog in their home. Some veterinary clinics have technicians that will take care of pets, or they may know of someone who will. For more information on Pet Sitting, contact NAPPS—National Association of Professional Pet Sitters, 1200 G Street, NW Suite 760, Washington DC, 20005.

If your Maltese is a show dog, you will need to find a person who can care for his coat as well as his everyday needs. Do not depend on someone who is not knowledgeable about the coat care. Your dog's breeder may be willing to help you during this time or, if not, may recommend someone who can.

Boarding a Maltese can be pretty scary because most boarding kennels are not set up to replicate the home environment. They are usually concrete runs with outdoor exercise areas. If you find you must board your Maltese, ask your veterinarian for a good recommendation. Visit the place where you will leave your dog before you actually take him there. Ask what their requirements are (proof of vaccinations, what vaccinations are necessary and so on) and ask for a tour of the facilities. Make sure you know what they do about flea control. If your dog suffers from flea-bite allergy, he can get in trouble at a boarding kennel.

A Maltese, especially if the coat is left long, will need to be groomed daily while you are gone. Find out if this boarding kennel provides that service for you.

FINDING THE DOG SHOW

Kennel clubs are located all over the country. On any given weekend, there are many dog shows to choose from in a variety of places. The American Kennel Club publishes a monthly *Schedule of Events* magazine that is part of the *AKC Gazette*, their official journal. This can help in determining where you would like to enter your dog because it contains a list of the upcoming shows. It also contains the names and addresses of superintendents, or show secretaries, who are licensed to oversee the show. The closing date for entries to a show is usually about two-and-one-half weeks before the actual show. Point-show fees may vary, and there is a fee for each class in which you enter your dog. You may want to write to these superintendents

Every weekend there are many kennel club shows held all over the country. Here, Jere Olson exhibits a Group-winning Maltese for Carol Frances Andersen. (Photo by Lloyd Olson Studios)

Attending a dog show will require that you travel. Some shows can be easily reached by car or van. Some exhibitors travel in a motor home and take along their own lodging! Shows that are great distances away may require air travel. The premium list is the information booklet sent out by the show secretary or super-intendent. This booklet contains informa-tion about the dog show including the name and location of the kennel club's event, the judges assigned to the Breeds, Groups and Best in Show and an entry form or two for that particular show. It will sometimes list trophies and other pertinent information. The entries will have a deadline date, after which no more entries can be received. Your entries will be processed by the superintendent or secretary, and confirmation will be sent back to you. With this confirmation will be a schedule for the day and, most of the time, a map so you can get to the show. Hotels and motels in the area that accept dogs will also be listed on the premium list or schedule. Make your plans ahead of time because there is usually not an abundance of motels that will accommodate you, and there will be many other exhibitors trying to find a place to stay.

and ask to be put on their mailing list. They usually only mail you entries for upcoming shows within a certain radius of where you live unless you request otherwise

All the rules and information concerning con-formation shows may be obtained by contacting the American Kennel Club. It is a wise idea to become familiar with the rules because they change periodically. For instance, you should know that a dog cannot become a Champion of Record with a limited registration or if the dog is spayed or neutered.

Looking Your Best in the Ring

Keeping in mind that you are a background for your dog and that you want the judge to notice the dog more than he notices you, plan your

To exhibit in conformation, one of the things your dog must be trained to do is stand on the table for examination by the judge in the ring. (Photo by Larry Abbott)

or a skirt and jacket. Pants suits can also look very appropriate. Consider the color of your dog when choosing your outfit. You are showing a white dog that will probably not show up very well if you select white or light-colored apparel. Remember

Your dog will be judged while he is moving as well as being examined on the table, so it is a good idea to have comfortable shoes that will not slip on the grass or on slick surfaces. (Photo by Larry Abbott)

wardrobe accordingly. It is a good idea to know where the show you plan to attend is located, what the weather is going to be like and whether you will be exhibiting your dog inside or outside.

Sudden changes in temperature can occur, so it is wise to carry a sweater or a jacket with you. You need to be free to move or, in the case of showing the Maltese, able to kneel down in whatever you choose to wear. Pockets are an asset in the ring for carrying a brush, a comb or some bait. Men usually wear a jacket with a nice shirt and tie or a sport-type shirt underneath. Women wear a dress

The beautiful coat that makes the Maltese easy to distinguish from other breeds is depicted here by the top winning Ch. Sand Island Small Kraft Lite, bred and owned by Carol Frances Andersen. (Photo courtesy of Vicki Abbott)

Which one is the better Toy to have? The one with all the personality, of course! Scrapper is owned by Larry and Vicki Abbott and Joseph Joly III. (Photo by Gay Glazbrook)

Ch. Shanlyn's Sparks R Fly'n relaxes in the sunshine and is a perfect example of the calm temperament of the Maltese. (Photo by Lynda Podgurski)

A Maltese was the companion of royalty long ago, and it is easy to see why the breed was so esteemed down through history. (Photo by Perry Struse)

The gentle, loving attitude of the Maltese is what makes him so endearing to his owner. Tag is Suzanne Johnston's very special boy. (Photo by Scott)

No matter what ring he's in, the Maltese certainly attracts attention! (Photo by Taylor Taylor)

Although Scrapper is small in comparison to his Australian Shepherd friend Flapjack, his sturdy Maltese physique can hold its own as a companion and as a playmate to larger dogs. (Photo by Missy Yuhl)

Serenade has learned that being a Toy is not so un-bearable! (Photo by Taylor Taylor & Mariko Sukezaki)

The Maltese has a clownish, endearing temperament, whether going for a spin in a toy car (above) or performing his own special magic (left)! (Photo above by Crisandra Maltese & Paulette; photo at left by Alex Smith)

While you might think of giving a Maltese for a Christmas present, it is a wiser idea to bring a new member of the family home at a time when he can have your undivided attention. (Photo by Vicki Abbott)

Ever playful, Maltese are always ready for a party—and to be the star of the show! (Photo courtesy of Andrea Noel)

Both as an adult (top) and as a puppy (bottom), a Maltese will provide friendship and delight. (Photos courtesy of Sandra Kenner & Chris Pearson)

Refined, gentle and adorable, the Maltese is a special companion. (Photo by Missy Yuhl & Ellie and Dick Merget)

to carry along a lint brush to remove any hair or dirt from your clothing before you enter the ring. Find comfortable walking shoes to wear that will not be distracting to the judge or to your dog. They should have rubber or crepe soles to keep you from slipping and being injured.

Remember that your little Maltese is walking down by your feet. If you are wearing heels that make a lot of noise, this will be very distracting to him. Jewelry that hangs loose, jangles or gets in the way is not to be worn in the ring. It can distract and even spook your dog at an inappropriate moment. Sometimes even a small necklace can get tangled up in your show lead when you put the lead around your neck while your dog is on the table. Overall, if you are as particular about your appearance as you are about your dog's grooming, you will present a total winning picture.

Maltese and handler—a total winning picture. (Photo by Michelle Perlmutter)

(photo by Brenda Morris)

CHAPTER TEN

Broadening Your Perspectives with Your Maltese

The opportunities are endless when it comes to being involved with your Maltese, no matter what your age. Maltese have been at the forefront of all kinds of performance competitions, and they are ambassadors of good will in therapy programs across the country. There are even Maltese that are trained as Hearing Assistance Dogs. Whatever you choose for your Maltese to do, he is up to the task!

OBEDIENCE

Obedience can start out as simply training your dog to have a few manners. It can also develop into a wonderful hobby that many Maltese owners are very actively involved in.

The important thing to consider in choosing a breed for obedience is not necessarily the intelligence of the breed itself but the intelligence and trainability of the individual dog. Your Maltese may or may not be cut out for intensive obedience training, and you as the trainer must be dedicated to the patience and time it will take to accomplish whatever the goal is. When selecting a Maltese for competitive obedience training, you must make sure the dog is structurally sound because he will be performing jumps and other tasks that will require fitness. If the dog has a disability, this will not eliminate him from competition, but you will want to pay close attention to whether he experiences pain or discomfort in performing the exercises. The dog can become stubborn because what he is doing is not a pleasant situation.

Scylla's Electric Oops A Daisy holds a CD title in obedience. Cookie's proud owner and trainer is Lee Guzman, and Cookie was bred by Larry and Vicki Abbott. (Photo by Jeannette Maurer)

There are obvious advantages to training your dog in obedience. The once unruly, hard-to-get-along-with dog can become a treasured companion and can avoid ending up in the humane society. The shy, more introverted companion can gain confidence and become more sociable. Whatever the level of need is, obedience training can be a fascinating sport. Your dog will love his training time spent with your undivided attention. And if you attend obedience classes, it can be fun to develop friendships with people who have a common interest.

The American Kennel Club acknowledged obedience around 1936. This competition has changed tremendously over the years even though many of the exercises remain the same. The Maltese is definitely a breed that can obtain these

titles, and many have been successful. The training of Maltese for the obedience ring began around the 1940s in the United States. Mr. Herb Kellogg, a former president of the American Maltese Association and an obedience enthusiast and judge, was the first person to place a CDX title on a Maltese. The Maltese was Kellogg's Beau, CDX. Other early obedience enthusiasts were Blanche Carlquist, with the first and fourth Maltese to earn UD titles, and Dr. Helen Poggi, with six Champion CD Maltese.

Obedience is a very competitive sport at dog shows today. There will usually be an obedience club in your area, and they may hold their trial in connection with the all-breed kennel club show.

When you are preparing your puppy or dog for an obedience title, matches can be very helpful. A fun match will be more flexible about allowing you to make corrections in the ring, and this is good practice. At the AKC Sanctioned Obedience matches, you are not allowed to make these corrections in the ring.

In obedience competition, it is possible for quite a few exhibitors to come home as winners if they earn a qualifying score. Most of the obedience titles are awarded after earning three qualifying scores, or *legs*. These must be won under three different judges. A perfect score is 200, which is extremely rare for a dog to accomplish. There are class exercises that the dog must do correctly, and each of the exercises has its own point value. A leg is earned after receiving a score of at least 170 and at least 50 percent of the points available in each exercise. The titles are Companion Dog (CD), Companion Dog Excellent(CDX) and Utility Dog (UD).

Any obedience Maltese knows you have to retrieve to get a CDX title! (Photo by Julie Phillips)

Amethyst, a very tiny Maltese, is quite well-known around the obedience ring with her owner and trainer Sandy Ferguson. She is pictured here winning at the AMA National Specialty in 1992. (Photo by Paulette)

To achieve a Companion Dog title (CD), your dog must accomplish the following exercises: heel on leash and figure eight (40 points), stand for examination (30 points), heel free (40 points), recall (30 points), long sit for one minute (30 points) and long down for three minutes (30 points).

To achieve a Companion Dog Excellent title (CDX), the following exercises are required: heel off leash and figure eight (40 points), drop on recall (30 points), retrieve on flat surface (20 points), retrieve over high jump (30 points), broad jump (20 points), long sit for three minutes out of sight (30 points) and long down for five minutes out of sight (30 points). Class exercises for a Utility Dog (UD) title are as follows: signal exercise (40 points), scent discrimination—article one (30 points), scent discrimination—article 2 (30 points), directed retrieve (30 points), moving stand and examination (30 points) and directed jumping 40 points).

After achieving the UD title, your dog may go on to the UDX and OTCh. UDX is Utility Dog Excellent, which went into effect in 1994. This title requires qualifying simultaneously ten times in Open B and Utility B but not necessarily at consecutive shows. The OTCh is the Obedience Trail Champion. This is awarded when a dog with his UD goes on to earn 100 championship points, a first place in Utility, a first place in Open and another first place in either class. The placements must be won under three different judges at all-breed obedience trials. The points are determined by the number of dogs competing in the Open B and Utility B classes.

There are three tracking titles that can be obtained: Tracking Dog (TD), Tracking Dog Excellent (TDX) and Variable Surface Tracking (VST). If all three titles are obtained, the dog becomes a Champion Tracker (CT).

Many people prefer tracking to obedience and some do both. Consider the fact that a small dog is

Am I too little for this jump? Obviously not, as many Maltese have achieved their CDX titles and more. (Photo by Julie Phillips)

closer to the ground, where it is easy to put his nose down to sniff. Tracking training encourages sniffing, so it might be better to achieve the obedience titles first with your Maltese.

Here are some tips if you are interested in obedience training:

- A good place to watch for Maltese in obedience besides an all-breed show is the American Maltese Association National Specialty, which has an obedience trial as part of the show.

- If you are interested in showing in obedience, it is a good idea to obtain a copy of the AKC Obedience regulations.

- Check on getting involved in obedience-training classes held by the local obedience club or by experienced obedience handlers.

- The sooner and the younger you can get your puppy into training classes, the easier it will be to train him. However, it is never too late to teach your dog something new!

Brenda Morris and Dewey run the agility course together. This sport can be a lot of fun for Maltese and their owners. (Photo by Brenda Morris)

AGILITY

Agility is extremely popular in England and Canada, and it is growing in popularity in the United States. It was first introduced by John Varley in England in 1978 to entertain the crowds between events at Crufts Dog show. However, Peter Meanwell, competitor and judge, actually developed the idea. The AKC acknowledged agility in August 1994. A dog must be 12 months of age to be entered. This is a team sport—the dogs, handlers and spectators can get involved! The handler either runs with his dog or positions himself on the course and directs his dog with verbal and hand signals. The course contains tunnels, jumps, chutes, tires, a pause table, an A-frame, a teeter-totter or seesaw and a balance beam with ramps.

The judge designs the course, which is set up and measured for distance. Times are set according to the level of the dog. A Novice level Maltese would have to complete the course at 2 yards per second, an Open level at 2.25 yards per second and an Excellent level at 2.5 yards per second. The AKC titles that can be earned in agility are Novice Agility Dog (NAD), Open Agility Dog (OAD), Agility Dog Excellent (ADX) and Master Agility Excellent (MAX). To acquire an agility title, the dog must earn a qualifying score in his respective class on three separate occasions under two different judges. The MAX is awarded after earning ten qualifying scores in the Agility Excellent Class.

The first agility trial in the United States was held in Houston, Texas, and was attended by a Maltese named Stanley. The first class to be judged was the Excellent class, and Stanley was the first dog on the line to be judged. Having a perfect run, Stanley was thus the first dog ever in AKC's history to earn a 100 score in agility! His full name is Springtime Stanley J-CDX, MX, AXJ, AAD, CGC, TDI, and he is owned by Marilyn Jensen. Brenda Morris is one of this breed's biggest agility supporters. Her first champion was

Dewey, bred by Peggy Wanner, shows off his expertise on the agility course. He is always trained and shown by his owner, Brenda Morris. (Photo by Brenda Morris)

There are many obstacles to overcome on the agility course, but a little Maltese seems to take it all in stride! (Photo courtesy of Brenda Morris)

homebred and won the 1976 AMA Sweepstakes. She started doing obedience in the early 1980s with Ch. Brenda's Fancy Annie O'Glenn CDX and stayed active in that sport. After serving as the chair for AMA Obedience and the Vegas Valley Obedience Club, Brenda put other things aside to become an active participant and supporter of agility for Maltese. Brenda currently shows Ch. Kandu's Thistle Dew Nicely CD, AX, OAJ, NADAC NC, ASCA Novice MA, CGC.

One of the main drawbacks to agility is finding a place to train. The obstacles take up a lot of space, and it is very time-consuming to put up and take down courses. More and more agility groups are becoming available as word spreads about the sport. Contact your local kennel club or look up agility on the Internet to find out where you can get information if you are interested in getting involved with your Maltese. (Information is also located in Appendix A.) Agility demonstrations sometimes are planned around the weekend of the American Maltese Association National Specialty Show. Check the breed club Web site for information.

JUNIOR SHOWMANSHIP

To be eligible for Junior Showmanship class, you must be at least 10 years of age and not older than 18. This competition is a wonderful way for young people to get experience and gain self-confidence in the ring. Frequently, Junior Showmanship is the

Springtime Stanley J has quite an impressive list of agility titles and has the distinction of being the first dog to ever earn a 100 score in agility in the United States. (Photo by Marilyn Jensen)

starting point for many successful exhibitors and handlers of the future.

The Junior in the ring is judged solely on his ability and skills in presenting his dog. The conformation of the dog is not taken into account by the judge. However, the condition of the dog as well as the grooming may be a reflection on the Junior handler.

Our eldest daughter, Tara, became interested in Junior Showmanship at an early age because she was always at dog shows with the family. She started out with a larger breed and, with training and dedication, made it into the Junior Showmanship finals at Westminster with the dog. When one of our very nice Maltese puppies decided he wouldn't walk for mom, Tara insisted that she could train him and finish his championship. Four majors later, she did exactly that, and Grammy became her dog for Junior Showmanship. They placed in

Tara is an example of what Juniors can do with a Maltese if they are willing to dedicate the time necessary for the training and grooming. (Photo by Don Petrulis Photography)

the top five Juniors in the country for a number of years, and Tara groomed every hair as well as helping us with our dogs.

The specific rules for Junior Showmanship have changed over the years. For the most updated rules, contact the American Kennel Club for their Junior Showmanship booklet.

Junior Showmanship classes are usually divided by age. The age is determined by the handler's age on the day of the show. Classes for Junior Showmanship are Novice Junior, Open Junior, Novice Senior and Open Senior. Novice Junior is for those at least 10 years of age and under 14 years of age. They must *not*, at the time of entry closing, have won three first places in a Novice Class at a licensed or member show. Open Junior is also for those at least 10 and under 14, but they must have won at least three

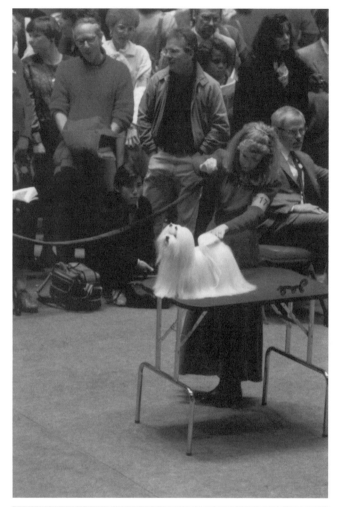

Westminster Kennel Club competition is a highlight for Junior Showmanship in this country. Tara exhibited Grammy in this competition in 1988. (Photo by Michelle Perlmutter)

first places in a Novice Junior Showmanship Class at a licensed or member show with competition present. Novice Senior is for those at least 14 years of age and under 18 years of age. They must *not*, at the time of entry closing, have won three first places in a Novice Class at a licensed or member show. Open Senior is also for those 14 and under 18, but they must have won at least three first places in a Novice Junior Showmanship Class at a licensed or member show with competition present.

Junior handlers must include their AKC Junior Handler number on each show entry and must remember to obtain this ahead of time from the AKC. Some Junior handlers and their parents take this competition very seriously, and others are just there for a good time and a learning experience. Success is measured in terms of wins. It is always advisable to obtain a dog for this competition that will be a very trainable dog. A Junior handler with a Maltese can do very well in this competition if he is willing to spend the time on the training and grooming.

CANINE GOOD CITIZEN

The Canine Good Citizen program is sponsored by the American Kennel Club. The purpose of this program is to encourage dog owners to train their dogs. Local clubs (usually in conjunction with a show) provide the pass/fail tests, and the dogs that pass are awarded a Canine Good Citizen Certificate. The test includes:

1. Accepting a friendly stranger
2. Sitting politely for petting
3. Appearance and grooming
4. Walking on a loose leash
5. Walking through a crowd
6. Sit and down on command/staying in place
7. Coming when called
8. Reaction to another dog
9. Reactions to distractions
10. Supervised separation

Obviously, the ideal situation would be for all pet owners to train their dogs for these few basic exercises, which would greatly decrease the need for so many humane shelters. Proof

of vaccination is required for your dog to participate in this event.

IMPORTANT DETAILS

It is important to know what the rules and limitations are for being able to enter your dog in certain activities. Obedience, tracking and agility allow purebred dogs with an Indefinite Listing Privilege (ILP) number, or a limited registration, to be exhibited and earn titles. The American Kennel Club's monthly *Events* magazine that is part of the *AKC Gazette* has a list of the upcoming obedience, tracking and agility events and the superintendent or secretary handling the show. You can write to these superintendents that are listed and ask to be put on their mailing list. They usually only mail you entries for upcoming shows within a certain radius of where you live unless you request otherwise.

All information on the rules and regulations for conformation shows or obedience trials may be obtained by contacting the American Kennel Club.

THE IMPORTANCE OF THE THERAPY DOG

Many breeds of dogs are currently becoming Registered Therapy Dogs, but no breed more loving than a Maltese. These dogs are taken by their owners into hospitals, elder day-care centers and nursing homes to provide therapy in a special form of love and companionship that only they can provide. This type of contact can be more helpful in a patient's recovery than any medication that could be prescribed. Studies of the human/animal bond point out the importance of the unique relationships that exist between people and pets.

A recent nationwide survey conducted by a leading pet-food manufacturer gauged just how important pets are in our lives. Here is what the survey found:

- 76 percent allow their pets to sleep on their beds

- 78 percent think of their pets as their children

- 84 percent display photos of their pets, mostly in their homes

- 100 percent talk to their pets

- 97 percent think their pets understand what they are saying

Is it any wonder that these little dogs can have a therapeutic effect on the people they come in contact with?

There are several organizations in all areas of the country that certify dogs for the Registered Pet Therapy Program. A few of these are the Delta Society, Therapy Dogs International and Therapy Dogs Incorporated. Your dog must be well-behaved to qualify for this type of work, and he will probably be required to pass the Canine Good Citizen test. When you own a therapy dog, it requires a

certain amount of commitment. You will make routine visits to the care-giving facility. The patients look forward to these visits and come to depend on them greatly. Therapy work can be very rewarding. Remember our little agility dog named Stanley? Well, he is a dog of many talents, as he is also a Registered Therapy Dog. From 1987 to 1995, Stanley worked his magic at nursing homes and elder day-care centers visiting patients twice a week before he retired to become the official mascot for Marilyn's son's soccer team! Contact one of these organizations in your area if you are interested in becoming involved in this type of work with your Maltese.

Maltese can be trained for many types of assistance. Willy is a hearing assistant for Rosemarie Saccardi. (Photo by Rosemarie & Ray Saccardi)

ASSISTANCE MALTESE

A Maltese can be trained to assist his owner in a variety of special ways. There are a number of organizations that work with owners with special disabilities. They teach the dogs and the owners to work together as a team to allow the owners more flexibility and independence in their lives. These organizations usually have strict requirements for the dogs that are trained. The dog's temperament must be ideal for this type of service.

One example of how a little Maltese can make a big difference is the story of a Hearing Impaired Training Dog named Willy. Scylla's Jo-Li Lite My Fire, or Willy, as he is affectionately called by his owner, Rosemarie Saccardi, was born at our house with great aspirations of being a great show dog. We met Rosemarie and her husband Ray on a November day in 1994 at a dog show in Maryland, and we learned that they were looking for an ideal Maltese with a very special purpose. Rosemarie has a hearing disability due to nerve damage as a child that allows her to hear only over a severely limited frequency range.

Since this condition could not be helped by surgery or a hearing aid, she was looking for a dog to train as her assistant. Willy was about 13 months

Sometimes a guy just has to go to work and wait to play until later! (Photo by Rosemarie & Ray Saccardi)

old at the time, and we could not think of a better place for him to be! So off he went, and after being trained by Canine Hearing Companions, a non-profit organization that trains dogs for this purpose, Willy became Rosemarie's constant companion and extra set of ears. He tells her when the oven timer goes off or the doorbell rings. He warns her when the phone rings or if someone approaches her from behind. Willy not only helps Rosemarie hear, he is also a wonderful companion and loves to go everywhere with her and Ray—especially to the beach! If you are specifically interested in the Canine Hearing Companion Program, you can write to them at: Canine Hearing Companions, Inc., 247 E. Forest Grove Road, Vineland, NJ 08360.

This is only one success story out of many that exemplifies the Maltese heart. There are many assistance programs and schools that train dogs to be valuable assets to their owners. Guide Dogs for the Blind, Canine Companions for Independence and Hearing Dogs for the Deaf are but a few of the organizations responsible for the training of these dogs—enriching the lives of disabled persons by making daily living just a little bit easier.

(photo by Callea Photo)

CHAPTER ELEVEN

The Maltese Headliners

There is nothing more stunning to watch than a beautifully structured Maltese in his glorious white coat floating effortlessly around the show ring. It is, needless to say, an attention grabber and has been the key to the consistent success of this breed at dog shows for years. Although we will attempt to point out some of the Maltese with historical significance in the conformation and obedience rings, it should be said that an abundance of Maltese have done their share of winning over the last thirty years or so. Grooming this breed is not an easy task. The fact that Maltese are recognized so significantly in the Toy Group is a tribute to the dedicated owners, breeders and handlers, as they have been very instrumental in the breed's notoriety.

THE LADIES

Ch. Co-Ca-He's Aennchen's Toy Dancer

When discussing the headliners in this breed, one must go back to the first Maltese to really "get the headlines" so to speak.

Ch. Co-Ca-He's Aennchen's Toy Dancer was exhibited to her many wins by her 15-year-old owner, Anna Marie Stimmler. In 1964, *Toy* was the first Maltese in history to ever win the Toy Group at Westminster Kennel Club. She was the top winning Maltese in 1964, achieving the record for Bests in Show for a Maltese. Toy won the very first American Maltese Association Specialty under William L.

Kendrick and went on to win the Toy Group on that day at Columbiana Kennel Club.

Ch. Aennchen's Poona Dancer

In February 1964, a female puppy was chosen from a litter out of Ch. Aennchen's Siva Dancer that would illuminate the pathway for all Maltese to

Ch. Aennchen's Poona Dancer with Frank Oberstar handling, winning the Toy Group at Westminster Kennel Club in 1966. (Photo by William P. Gilbert)

come in the toy ring. Ch. Aennchen's Poona Dancer, owned by Frank Oberstar and Larry Ward of Starward Maltese, won 38 Bests in Show and 131 Group Firsts during her illustrious career. Frank, Larry and Poona were a team that remains unsurpassed in this century. In 1966, Poona pranced to the top spot in the Toy Group at Westminster, making her the second Maltese in history to do so. She won the 1967 and 1968 American Maltese Association Specialties and was the very first Maltese to be awarded the Quaker Oats Award for the Top Group Winning Toy (1967). Poona was retired in 1968 upon winning the first Best in Show for a Maltese that year. Frank Oberstar went on to become a world-renowned judge and was well-respected as a Maltese expert. Larry Ward is a charter member and former President of the American Maltese Association and has remained supportive and active with the breed as an AMA board member.

Ch. Pendleton's Jewel

History was made again when, three years in a row (1969, 1970 and 1971), the American Maltese Association National Specialty was won by a beautifully presented bitch, Ch. Pendleton's Jewel. Dottie White was the owner and handler of Doll. Doll was acquired from Mrs. Ann Pendleton and was the Top Toy for two years, 1969 and 1970. In 1969, she was the second Maltese to achieve the Quaker Oats Award. Doll had twenty-eight Bests in Show to her credit and was a Best of Breed winner and Group placer at Westminster. She was

Ch. Pendleton's Jewel, a three-time AMA Specialty winner, was bred by Ann Pendleton and owned and handled by Dottie White.

the first Maltese to win Best in Show at the Kennel Club of Philadelphia.

Ch. Russ Ann Petite Charmer

Anna Mae Hardy had been successful in breeding champion Maltese since 1962 and decided to add to her breeding program. She purchased a little bitch from Emma Taylor. Apparently, the little Charmer turned out to be all her name implied, and her first big win came at 6 months of age at the American Maltese Association National Specialty where she was Best in Sweepstakes under breeder Frank Oberstar. In 1974, she was shown only eight months and became the Number One

Maltese Bitch for that year. She also was Best of Opposite Sex at the National Specialty. Retiring to become a mother in 1975, she produced a number of champions before returning to the ring at the National Specialty in 1978. There she won the Veteran Bitch Class and was chosen Best of Opposite Sex over seventeen champion bitches. She produced five litters before she was through and made history by becoming the Top Producing Best in Show Maltese Bitch of all time.

Ch. Malone's Snowy Roxann

Ch. Malone's Snowy Roxann was a very beautiful, lovely coated bitch that caught everyone's eye in the late 1970s. Roxann was owned by Nancy Shapland and was handled by Peggy Hogg. She tallied up fifty-one Bests in Show and fifty-two Group Firsts during her short career. She was a multiple Specialty winner and won Best of Breed at Westminster Kennel Club twice. Tragically, Roxann died during a cesarean section on her first litter. She left three daughters behind, one of which (Roseann) became a multiple Group and Best in Show winner shown by Peggy. The other two girls also finished their championships, making for an all-champion litter.

Ch. Gemmery's Citrine Bean

Ch. Russ Ann Petite Charmer held the record for the Top Producing Best in Show bitch in the breed until *Bee* came along. Ch. Gemmery's Citrine Bean was a daughter of Ch. Martin's Sweet Bean Puff, ROM, owned by Daryl Martin. Bee, shown by

Daryl, obtained four Bests in Show and twenty Group Firsts in less than a year (1981). She then retired to the whelping box to produce eight champions, beating the record previously held by Anna Mae Hardy's bitch.

Ch. Melodylane Sings O'Al-Mar Luv

Serenade was purchased from Freeman and Mary Purvis (Melodylane Maltese) in 1992 for Mariko Sukezaki of Japan. Melodylane Maltese has produced many Best in Show and Group winning Maltese, including Best in Show Ch. Melodylane

The 1993 AMA National Specialty was won by Serenade, who was owned by Mariko Sukezaki and David and Sharon Newcomb and was bred by Marjorie Lewis. (Photo by Booth Photography)

Lite N' Lively Luv, the dam to the top winning Maltese dog of all time—Ch. Sand Island Small Kraft Lite.

Mariko Sukezaki, of MerryDance Maltese, visited us at the American Maltese Association National Specialty in 1991 and expressed an interest in acquiring a Maltese to show in the United States. After purchasing some of Carol Andersen's dogs while Henry was being shown, Mariko obtained Serenade and started her career. Serenade was bred by Marjorie Lewis of Al-Mar fame. She is a combination of Marjorie's breeding and the Myi and Melodylane lines. Although only shown for about sixteen months, Serenade achieved twelve Bests in Show and three Maltese Specialty wins including the American Maltese Association National Specialty in 1993 under breeder judge Frank Oberstar. Out of the 103 Bests of Breed that she accomplished, she won 56 Group Firsts and 36 other Group placements. When finished with her career, Serenade returned to her owner in Japan to become a mother and a pampered pet.

Ch. Ta Jon's Tickle Me Silly

This little girl was shown in the late 1990s. She was owned by Sam and Marion Lawrence and was bred by John and Tammy Simon. Her unforgettable career began when she won Winners Bitch and Best of Winners at the American Maltese Association National Specialty in 1995, and she retired after winning Best of Opposite Sex at Westminster in 1999. Known for her outgoing Maltese personality, during her years as a Special she obtained a record-breaking 103 Bests in Show and 262 Group Firsts. Her other accomplishments include winning two National Specialties (1996 and 1997) and winning Best of Breed at Westminster as well as placing in the Group.

THE GENTLEMEN

Ch. Joanne-Chen's Maya Dancer

Ch. Joanne-Chen's Maya Dancer was bred by Joanne Hesse, was owned by Joe and Mamie Gregory and was handled throughout his career by Peggy Hogg. His impressive show career includes

winning 43 Bests in Show, 134 Group Firsts, and the Toy Group at Westminster in 1972, making him the third Maltese in history to do so. He won the 1972 American Maltese Association National Specialty and that year went on to win the Toy Group and Best In Show over 3,975 dogs at International Kennel Club, which included the specialty. He was presented with the Quaker Oats Award for Top Group Winning Toy in 1971 and 1972.

Ch. Stan-Bar's Spark of Glory

Only shown about five shows per year, Sparky ranked among the top Maltese from 1976 to 1984. He took his place in history when he became the oldest toy dog to win an all-breed Best in Show!

Peggy Hogg handled Ch. Joanne-Chen's Maya Dancer to his many prestigious wins for owners Joe and Mamie Gregory. (Photo by Shafer)

Ch. Stan-Bar's Spark of Glory was still winning Best in Shows at almost 10 years of age. Sparky is shown winning the Toy Group under breeder-judge Frank Oberstar with his owner and handler, Beverly Passe.

This was three months shy of his 10th birthday. Owned by Beverly Passe of the House of Myi Maltese, Sparky passed his temperament, soundness and heart down to his children and grandchildren. Sparky produced about thirty champions, and many of the nation's top winning Maltese carry Sparky's name in the back of their pedigree.

Three of his top winning relatives include Ch. Keoli's Small Kraft Warning, Ch. Sand Island Small Kraft Lite, and Ch. Melodylane Songs O'Al-Mar Luv.

Am. Can. Bda. Ch. Oak Ridge Country Charmer

Charmer caught everyone's eye in the late 1970s. He was breeder-owner handled by Carol A. Neth,

Ch. Oak Ridge Country Charmer won this AMA National Specialty in 1977 as well as the one in 1979. Carol Neth was his breeder, owner and handler. (Photo by Bernard Kernan)

completing his career with twenty-three Bests in Show and ninety Group Firsts (192 Group Placements out of 237 Best of Breeds). He won the American Maltese Association National Specialty two times, in 1977 and 1979. He was Best in Show at the Montreal, Quebec Show and the International Show of Shows. Charmer was a Top Producer as well with twenty-seven champions including a multiple Best in Show daughter.

Ch. Joanne-Chen's Mino Maya Dancer

The late 1970s heralded another Dancer bred by Joanne Hesse. Mino was owned by Mrs. Blanche Tenerowicz and was handled to his wins by Daryl Martin. He achieved a record of 34 Bests in Show and 150 Group Firsts, which set the Group record for the breed since Ch. Aennchen's Poona Dancer. Mino was the Top Maltese in 1977, 1979 and 1980. He was the Top Toy Dog and the Quaker Oats Winner for the Top Group Winning Toy Dog in 1980. He won the American Maltese Association National Specialty in 1980 and again in 1981—a historical moment—when his win was from the Veteran's Class! Mino produced many champions and left a very large legacy of top winning children and grandchildren.

Ch. Non-Vel's Weejun

The Top Maltese in 1984 was Ch. Non-Vel's Weejun, owned by Candace Mathes-Gray and Mary Senkowski. Weejun was handled throughout his impressive career by Bill Cunningham. A very

A beautiful portrait of Ch. Joanne-Chen's Mino Maya Dancer, owned by Blanche Tenerowicz and handled by Daryl Martin.

stylish dog, he accumulated over eleven Bests in Show, fifty Group Firsts and many other placements. He was Best of Breed at Westminster Kennel Club in 1984 and won Best of Breed at the American Maltese Association National Specialty in 1985.

Ch. Scylla's Mina Maya Starfire

At Scylla Maltese in the early 1980s, we bred what ended up being a little 5-pound dynamo. Ch. Scylla's Mina Maya Starfire was the grandson of Ch. Joanne-Chen's Mino Maya Dancer and the great-great grandson of Ch. Joanne-Chen's Maya Dancer. Starfire's lineage served him well. He

started his career going Winners Dog and Best of Winners at the American Maltese Association National Specialty in 1982 in Las Vegas and went on to achieve eight Bests in Show and forty-five Group Firsts, all breeder-owner handled. He was the Top Maltese in 1985, after which he retired to become a producer of champions himself. Starfire was co-owned by Audrey Drake of Toimanor Pekingese fame.

Ch. Keoli's Small Kraft Warning

When Carol Andersen (Sand Island Maltese) decided to add another breed to her already successful Skye Terriers, she purchased Ricky from Jeff and Molly Sunde. Ricky's background was from the House of Myi (Beverly Passe). Ricky was handled by Jackie Liddle Stacy in the mid 1980s, became a multiple Best in Show dog and won the Breed and Group Placements at Westminster Kennel Club. Perhaps what he is most noted for, however, is his prestigious Toy Group win at the AKC Centennial Show over approximately 1,000 other Toy Dogs.

Ch. C and M's Tootsey's Lolly Pop

C and M (Carole Thomas and Mary Day) breeding has been very influential across the country. Lolly was handled by Mary Day and was owned by Sherry Lemond Ray, Mary Day and Carole Thomas. Although shown on a limited basis, Lolly accumulated quite a record—six Bests in Show

Ch. Keoli's Small Kraft Warning won the prestigious AKC Centennial Toy Group, and he was a multiple Best in Show Maltese. Ricky was owned by Carol Frances Andersen. (Photo by Meyer)

Ch. C and M's Tootsey's Lolly Pop won the AMA National Specialty in 1988 and again in 1992. Lolly was bred by Mary Day and Carole Thomas and was owned by Sherry Lemond Ray and Mary and Carole. (Photo by Missy Yuhl)

and about thirty Group Firsts. He was a Best of Breed Winner twice at Westminster Kennel Club and won the American Maltese Association National Specialty in 1988 and again from the Veteran's Class in 1992. Lolly created a following wherever he went and became an outstanding producer.

Ch. Louan's Apache Starfire

Elsie Burke began breeding Maltese in 1979 and has produced numerous champions over the years. One of the most outstanding dogs at Louan's was Ch. Louan's Apache Starfire, a son of our Ch. Scylla's Mina Maya Starfire and Elsie's Ch. Louan's Apache Dancer. He finished quickly, we started his career, and he accumulated five Bests in Show,

twenty-one Group Firsts, and seventy-five other Group Placements in a little over a year. He was the Number One Maltese in 1988. Elsie has not only been involved in conformation but has also been an obedience exhibitor with her Maltese.

Ch. Sand Island Small Kraft Lite

Henry, a Maltese known for his beautiful type and movement, was the breathtaking result of a crossroads where years of sound breeding came together from different directions. I had the distinct honor of having handled him. He was bred and owned by Carol Frances Andersen, who also owned both his Best in Show father, Ch. Keoli's Small Kraft Warning (AKC Centennial Group winner), and his Best in Show mother, Ch.

Melodylane Lite N' Lively Luv. With the immeasurable help of her kennel manager, Jere Olson, the breeding of these two dogs produced a Maltese that will never be forgotten. Henry set new records for the breed at the time he was shown. He finished by going Best of Winners and Best of Opposite Sex over eight Dog Specials at Westminster in 1989, the last year that class dogs were exhibited at that show. He was the Top Maltese and Top Toy Dog in 1990 and 1991 with 82 Bests in Show and over 235 Group Firsts. Among his prestigious Best in Show wins were Tuxedo Park Kennel Club, Old Dominion Kennel Club and Ravenna Kennel Club. He was awarded with fifth place among all breeds in the Kennel Review Tournament of Champions in 1990.

Henry was only the second Maltese to be awarded two Quaker Oats Awards for Top Group Winning Toy Dog (1990 and 1991). He won two Science Diet Awards, being consistently in the top

Ch. Sand Island Small Kraft Lite, in 1992 under Dawn Vick Hansen, became only the fourth Maltese to ever win the Toy Group at Westminster Kennel Club. He was bred and owned by Carol Frances Andersen and was handled throughout his career by Vicki Abbott.

ten of all breeds. Added to this were five Specialty wins including two American Maltese Association Specialties (1990—the Silver Anniversary Specialty and 1991). He won Best of Breed at Westminster in 1990 and 1991, achieving a Group 3 and a Group 4. To top it all off, on the day he retired in 1992, he again won the Breed and entered the history books as only the fourth Maltese to ever win the Toy Group at Westminster.

Ch. Shanlyn's Rais'n A Raucous

Scrapper first became famous at the American Maltese Association National Specialty in 1992, when he went Winners Dog and Best of Winners handled from the Bred-By Class with his breeder Lynda Podgurski. He was not yet a year old. Lynda finished him with group placements, and then he came to live with us. Scrapper was owned throughout his career by Joseph Joly III, David and Sharon Newcomb and myself. Scrapper's first stop on the campaign trail was in January 1994 at The Kennel Club of Palm Springs, where he promptly went Best in Show (with his breeder getting more than a little excited outside the ring)! He was only campaigned for the 1994 year. He won Best of Breed at Westminster Kennel Club in 1994 and retired by winning Best of Breed at Westminster in 1995. In those short months, he accumulated twenty-seven Bests in Show and ninety Group Firsts, making him the Top Toy Dog for 1994. Out of 141 Best of Breeds, he won or placed in the Group 131 times and was the American Maltese Association National Specialty winner in 1994. He won a Science Diet Award for being in the Top Ten Dogs All-Breeds and the Pedigree Award for Top Maltese. Scrapper holds the record for the largest Best in Show ever won by a Maltese, the Evansville Kennel Club with close to 5,000 dogs entered.

Scrapper's career started off with a bang at 10 months of age when he went Winners Dog and Best of Winners at the AMA National Specialty from the Bred-By Class with his breeder, Lynda Podgurski. (Photo by Paulette)

AMERICAN MALTESE ASSOCIATION NATIONAL SPECIALTY WINNERS

Ch. Co-Ca-He's Aennchen's Toy Dancer—Anna Marie Stimmler, owner	1966
Ch. Aennchen's Poona Dancer—Frank Oberstar and Larry Ward, owners	1967
Ch. Aennchen's Poona Dancer—Frank Oberstar and Larry Ward, owners	1968
Ch. Pendleton's Jewel— Dorothy White, owner	1969
Ch. Pendleton's Jewel— Dorothy White, owner	1970
Ch. Pendleton's Jewel— Dorothy White, owner	1971
Ch. Joanne-Chen's Maya Dancer—Joe and Mamie Gregory, owners	1972
Ch. Mike Mars Sirius of Revlo—Mary Olver, owner	1973
Ch. Cara Maya's Mister— Shirley Hrabak, owner	1974

Ch. Celia's Mooney Forget Me Not—Pricilla Brown and Lara Olive, owners	1975	Ch. Sand Island Small Kraft Lite—Carol Frances Andersen, owner	1990
Ch. So Big's Desert Delight—Freda Tinsley, owner	1976	Ch. Sand Island Small Kraft Lite—Carol Frances Andersen, owner	1991
Ch. Oak Ridge Country Charmer—Carol and Tom Neth, owners	1977	Ch. C and M's Tootsey's Lolly Pop—Sherry LeMond Ray, Mary Day and Carole Thomas, owners	1992
Ch. Su Le's Jonina—Barbara Bergquist, owner	1978	Ch. Melodylane Sings O' Al-Mar Luv—Mariko Sukezaki and Sharon and David Newcomb, owners	1993
Ch. Oak Ridge Country Charmer—Carol and Tom Neth, owners	1979	Ch. Shanlyn's Rais'n A Raucous—Joseph Joly III, Sharon and David Newcomb and Vicki Abbott, owners	1994
Ch. Joanne-Chen's Mino Maya Dancer—Blanche Tenerowicz, owner	1980	Ch. Merri Paloma—Barbara Merrick and David Fitzpatrick, owners	1995
Ch. Joanne-Chen's Mino Maya Dancer—Blanche Tenerowicz, owner	1981	Ch. Ta-Jon's Tickle Me Silly—Samuel and Marion Lawrence, owners	1996
Ch. Rebecca's Desert Valentino—Freda Tinsley, owner	1982	Ch. Ta-Jon's Tickle Me Silly—Samuel and Marion Lawrence, owners	1997
Ch. Nobel Faith's White Tornado—Faith Knobel, owner	1983	Ch. Marcris Risque' Omen—Joyce Watkins, owner	1998
Ch. Myi's Ode to Glory Seeker—Beverly Passe, owner	1984	Ch. Showboat's Miss Piggy of C and M—Barbara Brown and Peter J. Rogers III, owners	1999
Ch. Non-Vel's Weejun—Candace Mathes and Mary Senkowski, owners	1985		
Ch. Villa Malta's Chicklett—Tom and Nancy Jennings, owners	1986		
Ch. Bar None Electric Horseman—Jackie and Keith Garber, owners	1987		
Ch. C and M's Tootsey's Lolly Pop—Sherry LeMond Ray, Mary Day and Carole Thomas, owners	1988		
Ch. Two Be's Hooked on Sugar—Betty Eaton and Billie Edwards, owners	1989		

MALTESE OBEDIENCE HEADLINERS

First CDX Title Kellogg's Beau, owned by Herb Kellogg

First UD Title Luce's Miss Lucy of Villa Malta (1963), owned by Blanche Carlquist

Second UD Title	Muff of Buckeye Circle, owned by Ida Marsland
Third UD Title	Whispering Pines Sweet Jill, owned by Inez Funk
Fourth UD Title	Caress of Winddrift, owned by Blanche Carlquist
First Ch. CDX and UD Title	Ch. Gulfstream Treasure, owned by Mary Lou Porlick
First TD Title	Joy's Mr. Feather, owned by Carol Kollander
Second TD Title	Dazzlyn Sir Frost, owned by E. Drobac
First UDT Title	Joy's Mr. Feather, owned by Carol Kollander
First High in Trial	Muff of Buckeye Circle, UD, owned by Ida Marsland
Second High in Trial	Caje's Razzle Dazzle Darling, owned by Carol Pressman
Most Obedience Titles Held by a Maltese	Joy's Mr. Feather, Am. UDT and TDX, Can. OB Ch. and TDX, Bermuda CDX and TD, Mexican T, owned by Carol Kollander
First Agility Maltese to Score 100	Springtime Stanley J CDX, MX, AXJ, AAD, TDI, owned by Marilyn Jensen

Lady Crisandra Suni Cristin UDX accumulated many awards including those given by the American Maltese Association for Top Obedience Maltese. Martha Tiller was her trainer and owner. (Photo courtesy of C. Pearson & S. Kenner)

AMERICAN MALTESE ASSOCIATION OBEDIENCE AWARDS

The American Maltese Association has within the last decade begun an Award for the Top Scoring Maltese Dog in Obedience.

In 1991, Ch. Merryland Mystic Maker CD, owned and trained by Faith Maciejewski, was the winner. Faith was an institution where Maltese obedience was concerned, having had much success with her Ch. Ginger Jake, CDX. Ginger Jake was in the top rankings in the country in the late 1970s and early 1980s. In 1992, the award went to Piccolo Elegante Gucci CDX, owned and trained by Julie Phillips. Julie has been a very active supporter of obedience within the American Maltese Association.

For 1993, honors went to Brenda's A-Dori-Bl-Dahl CDX, owned by Brenda Morris and Rita

Dahl and trained by Brenda. Brenda is a school-teacher from Nevada and is a prime example that your schedule is never too busy to train your Maltese. She has been instrumental in promoting agility for Maltese and is involved in training her own dogs for this event.

The Top AMA Obedience Maltese for 1994 was Lady Crisandra Suni Christine UD, owned and trained by Martha Tiller. This little achiever was also the winner for 1996. Martha has been very active in training more than one of her dogs in obedience. In 1995, the award went to Seven Star Tennessa Yahtzee CD, owned by Dee Hillyer, and the runners up were two dogs owned by Martha Tiller. Dee always looks like she is having such a great time in the ring with her dog! In 1997, Whitetails Iced Orchid CD, owned and trained by Bonnie Fruzen, was the award winner; in 1998, the award was given again to one of Martha Tiller's dogs—Mlle. Nicole Danielle UDX.

In 1979, one of the first obedience trials was held in conjunction with the American Maltese Association National Specialty since 1967. Entries in the CD or Novice Class numbered seven. There were six in Open (CDX), and three in Utility

(UD). Nat and Joan's (Lewis) Sugar Cookie CDX, a very little Maltese with a very big reputation in the South, earned a high score of $193\frac{1}{2}$. Ch. Ginger Jake CDX, owned and trained by Faith Maciezewski, tied Sugar Cookie's score. A run-off determined Ch. Ginger Jake CDX to be the winner—a very exciting day in the history of obedience at the AMA Specialty.

Sitting among his trophies is Piccolo Elegante Gucci CDX, owned and trained by Julie Phillips. Among his other awards, Gucci was an American Maltese Association Award winner. (Photo by Julie Phillips)

(Photo by Linda Lamoureux)

CHAPTER TWELVE

What You Should Know About Breeding Your Maltese

Breeding should be taken seriously and should be considered a quest for improvement, not a means of making money. Serious breeders make each breeding more exciting than the last one, always striving for healthier and better-quality dogs. The breeder from whom you purchase your puppy may request that you either spay or neuter the puppy because he does not want the offspring of his dogs bred indiscriminately. There may be an exception to this if you have obtained your puppy for show or if the breeder has agreed to allow you to breed the dog under his direct supervision.

By involving yourself in the breeding of dogs, you will have a big responsibility for the new lives you create. You must feed them, care for their medical needs, find ideal homes for them and on and on—it is a full-time occupation or hobby. Make sure you will have the time, dedication and finances that will be necessary before you proceed.

SPAYING OR NEUTERING YOUR MALTESE

If you or the breeder decide that your puppy will not be bred, you will want to set up an appointment with your veterinarian to have your puppy spayed or neutered. There are many benefits to

*When deciding to breed, you must be
dedicated to the new lives your create.
(Photo by Suzanne Johnston)*

having this surgery done at a young age, about
6 months old.

Unspayed females can develop mammary or
ovarian cancer or may end up with an infected
uterus (pyometra) later on in life. This can be
life-threatening and is unnecessary to risk. The
spaying is performed under general anesthetic
and is easier on a younger dog. If you have an
older dog that requires this surgery, it is a good
idea to run blood-screening and heart-function
tests to make sure that proceeding with the
surgery will not create any problems. During
heat cycles, females must be carefully kept away
from any males. They will sometimes urinate

frequently before and after their cycle, which may
require more effort and possibly cleanup on your
part.

Neutering involves removing the testicles but
leaving the scrotum of the dog. It is also performed
under general anesthetic. Sometimes Toy dogs can
retain testicles, and this can develop into cancer.
Unneutered males are at a risk for testicular cancer, perineal fistulas, perianal tumors and fistulas
and prostatic disease.

If neutered at 6 months of age, some behaviors
may be eliminated in the male before they start.
Hormonal aggressiveness can create behavior that
most owners will frown on. Dogs can hike their
legs to mark their territory, especially if there is a
female in heat around.

Some males, especially in this breed, are very
slow to mature as far as being hormonally aggressive. We have seen dogs as old as a year that have
never been bred and are still squatting like a female
to urinate. Your decision when to neuter will be
up to you and the puppy's breeder. If you purchase
your male at a little older age, this does not necessarily mean that you will have problems training
him or that he will have developed any "manly"
habits.

When choosing whether to purchase a male or
a female Maltese, one might think that some consideration needs to go into the personality of the
individual sex; however, with this breed, one sex
is not better or less of a problem than the other.
They are both equally loving, and the personality
depends on the individual puppy. Some of our
most loving and willing-to-please Maltese are
males.

Do not worry about your dog gaining a lot of weight or drastically changing personality after being neutered or spayed. This is usually not the case. Just make sure your dog gets an adequate amount of exercise and good food; if later in life he begins to gain a little weight, consult your veterinarian for a change in diet.

SHOULD YOU CHOOSE TO BREED

There is much to educate yourself about before you attempt to breed that first litter. Think about why you are choosing to embark on this new venture. Do you just want your children to experience the birth process? This is not a good reason—buy them a videotape; it's cheaper. Do you want to make a lot of money? Besides the fact that this

practice is looked down upon by serious breeders who are trying to improve the breed, you aren't going to get very far. Maltese normally have two or three puppies, and the veterinarian bills can outweigh any profits if a cesarean section is involved. Stud fees can also be incurred.

A serious breeder is thrilled if he breaks even, but he is willing to expend whatever it takes to produce great quality. There are too many puppy mills in this country that have multiple breeds, including Maltese, on the premises in an attempt at making money, usually without regard for improvement of the breeds or health issues. Unfortunately, it is the little dogs that ultimately suffer, and many of them end up in shelters or rescue organizations.

The one and only good reason to breed Maltese is to attempt to produce dogs of excellent quality, both in health and conformation. Your goal should be to improve the Maltese breed and to be responsible to the dogs you produce. If you can count yourself as part of this category, then proceed with your plans.

You will want to gain some practical knowledge about the selection of a dog for breeding, the mating process, taking care of a bitch in whelp and caring for the litter after it is born. Although there are several very good books on this subject, which you should definitely read and make part of your library, there is nothing better than a mentor who has been there and who can help you gain knowledge through his experience. The

A new breeder needs to be aware that a Maltese litter can consist of only two or three puppies and may involve a C-section or other veterinary bills. (Photo by Judy Crowe)

breeder of the dog you choose is an ideal person to go to for insight. Not only will he be able to help you understand the breeding process of the Maltese, he also can tell you about anything that might be particular to his line of dogs that you need to know.

Selecting the Perfect Bitch

Selecting a Maltese to breed should be similar to selecting a show dog in that you must be able to

Ch. Melodylane Lite N' Lively Luv, known as Lisa, was a multiple Best in Show bitch owned by Carol Frances Andersen. She is a very good example of what acquiring a quality bitch can do for a breeding program. Not only was she a winner in the ring, she also was the dam of the top winning Maltese dog of all time, Henry. In addition, she produced Ch. Sand Island Small Buoy Lite, known as Tyler, who is currently a top producer in the breed. (Photo by Missy Yuhl)

understand and interpret the AKC Breed Standard. Most breeders have learned through examining many specimens of the breed how to evaluate their dogs. You will need to find a breeder you can trust to help you in your selection. The bitch with whom you choose to start your breeding program will be what is called your *foundation bitch*, and she will need to be sound and of good quality. Do not skimp on the purchase of this foundation bitch.

To breed quality, you must start with quality. Breeders are sometimes reluctant to part with quality bitches into inexperienced hands. If you are fortunate enough to find a breeder who is willing to let you purchase what it has taken years for him to produce, spend the extra money now and you will pay out less in the long run. Follow his advice and trust that what he tells you comes from his many years of experience.

Selecting a Sire

A good time to look for a stud dog to breed to your bitch is not when she comes into season. This preparation must be done far in advance because the chosen stud dog may be very far away or may be in the process of being shown or campaigned. Attempt to learn as much as you can about the genetic background of your bitch so you can select the appropriate traits in a stud dog. Learn what the stud dog has produced, not only what the pedigree is or what he looks like. Most stud dogs, after having a number of litters, will show some consistent dominance of particular characteristics when bred to different bitches. Avoid breeding to a stud dog that you know carries the same faults as your bitch. Some people look for a very tiny dog to breed their bitch to for reduction of size of the puppies. This can be unfortunate because the tiny dog may be an exception to the rule in his line, and he may not produce smaller dogs. In fact, the opposite may occur. The sire that is consistent with producing a particular desired characteristic in most of his litters is the best choice.

The stud dog you choose should obviously be sound in body and in temperament. Never use a dog just because he is a big winner in the ring or because he is the most popular current stud. The dog you choose should be the one that will most likely compliment your bitch's characteristics.

Choose a stud dog based on what will compliment your bitch the best. Spend time investigating by talking with the breeders of the stud dogs you are considering. (Photo by Robin Tauber)

Since Maltese have only been in the AKC stud book for a little over 100 years, the top winning lines in the United States are often very closely related. When looking at the pedigree of a particular dog, realize that it is a printout of his genetic past. Look back as far as you can, at least five generations, and see what ancestors the dog may have in common with your bitch. If the common ancestors were top winners and producers, so much the better!

Different breeding choices can be made when it comes to mixing the genetics of two dogs. *Inbreeding* is the breeding of very closely related dogs—such as brother to sister, mother to son and so on—where they are not separated any further than one generation. This system of breeding should really only be used by experienced breeders with very high-quality stock. *Linebreeding* is the breeding of dogs that are closely related to a common ancestor but are probably not related to each other. The ancestor should be common to both the sire and the dam. *Outcrossing* is the breeding of dogs with no common ancestors, usually within five generations. Sometimes a breeder will deliberately outcross to bring in desirable qualities and to increase fertility and strength in his line.

Finally, talk to the breeder of your foundation bitch and get ideas for the best way to proceed with selecting an appropriate sire for your litter. Contact the owner of the sire to see if the stud dog will be available to breed to your bitch. Arrange everything ahead of time such as the shipping of your bitch, the required stud fee and contract or any tests the owner of the sire expects you to have done by your veterinarian prior to breeding.

Ch. Scylla's Mina Maya Starfire was a product of linebreeding. The common ancestor for his dam and sire was Ch. Joanne-Chen's Mino Maya Dancer. Obviously, this was a good choice, as Starfire became a top winner and producer. (Photo by Don Petrulis Photography)

The Mating Process

Before your bitch comes in season, it is a wise idea to make sure she has proper immunity by updating her on any vaccinations that may be necessary. Again, the protocols are changing relating to this, so check with your dog's breeder to see what is safest for your Maltese. Also make sure your bitch does not have any parasites that she could pass on to her puppies. Have your veterinarian examine her stool under a microscope because the eggs of some worms are not easy to detect. If you have your bitch on any medication for fleas or other conditions that would not be wise to continue

during breeding or pregnancy, you will want to take her off at this time. Some stud dog owners will require a brucellosis test done on your bitch. Brucellosis is a disease that is sexually transmitted and can ruin a stud dog, so it is a courtesy to the stud dog owner to comply with this request if made.

Usually, the first season on a bitch occurs anywhere from 6 to 9 months of age. Sometimes with toy breeds, and in some lines of Maltese, the first cycle will not occur until much later. Some can even wait until a year old. It is not wise to breed your puppy at her first season because she is still growing and her bones need all the nutrients to make her a strong and sound adult. By the second season, she should be ready to be bred. Some breeders who exhibit their breeding stock will wait even a little longer until the bitch has finished her championship.

The normal length of time between seasons is six months, but many Maltese can have a shorter or longer interval. Some bitches will cycle four months, then eight months, then four months again. It is a wise idea for the health of the bitch and the litters to skip a season between breedings. Your bitch needs to recuperate from raising a litter, especially a large one. (If you have a one-puppy litter and decide to breed twice in a row, rest your bitch the following season.)

When your bitch comes in season, the cycle will last for about twenty-one days. Specific changes occur during each phase of the cycle, and you will have to have some idea of when your bitch will ovulate in order for her to conceive. Testing can be done by your veterinarian to determine when this is about to occur. Vaginal smears are one way of determining what stage your bitch is in. A vaginal fluid sample is taken by inserting a cotton swab into the vagina, and the fluid is placed on a slide and viewed under a high-power microscope. Progesterone tests are the newest way of determining ovulation time. This requires a blood sample to test the levels of progesterone in the blood, which is better at determining the best time for breeding. Either of these procedures can eliminate the guesswork and can save you a lot of time and money, especially if you are shipping your bitch.

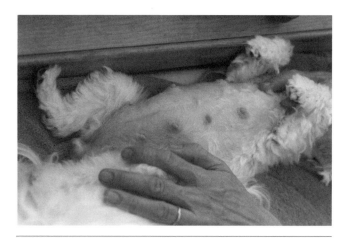

Ovulation timing can be tricky, but the results of spending a little extra effort in getting the testing done can result in a very pregnant Maltese! (Photo by Pamela Wang)

It has been reported that more bitches miss from being bred too early than from being bred too late, so patience is of the essence. Although the tests are a good indicator of the general ovulation time, your bitch may show her readiness in a more specific way. She may become more accepting to the male, and her vaginal discharge will probably change to a lighter color. The vulva will become softer and flabbier than it was at the beginning of her cycle. If all these conditions are right, and touching the vulva slightly will make the bitch switch her tail to one side, she has probably ovulated and is ready to breed.

If you plan to ship your bitch, get the results of the tests from your veterinarian about six to nine days into her season and have him make out a health certificate. This will be required to ship her on any major airline. It is a good idea to send the bitch to the stud dog a few days ahead of actual

breeding so she can settle in and not be stressed while being bred.

The stud dog owner is responsible for making sure the breeding is accomplished—he is not responsible for the bitch actually getting pregnant. Most breeders will offer a return breeding at no charge to a bitch that misses for some reason or another.

There are several reasons why a bitch might miss—the biggest is breeding at the wrong time. With these little Maltese, ovulation can be a tricky thing. Some will go out of the normal range of between the tenth and fourteenth days, when the normal time for ovulation occurs. We have seen bitches that will ovulate on as early as the fifth day or as late as the twenty-first day! So it is important to keep an eye on the bitch herself as well as doing the tests.

Other reasons might be stress or if there is an infection present. It is not a bad idea to have your bitch checked for any infections before she is bred. Your veterinarian can do a culture to determine what might be present so it can be treated beforehand. If the breeding cannot be accomplished naturally, it may be wise to do artificial insemination. This can be done by a veterinarian or a breeder educated in this procedure. Sometimes a bitch that has never been bred will become anxious or vicious, and this may be the only way of accomplishing the breeding without injuring the stud dog.

Your Maltese Male as a Stud Dog

I have received many phone calls from local Maltese owners who wish for someone, anyone, to breed to their dog. They, of course, think that Maltese breeders will just run to breed to their little male, and they want to know how to advertise to accomplish this! It is very hard to make them understand, if they are not involved in the breeding of dogs for the improvement of the breed, that this will just never happen. More often than not, it is the owner of the bitch that seeks out the particular stud dog, not the other way around.

Most breeders are looking for a specific type of dog for their bitch. They will seek out the known producers or a dog that is a linebreeding for their bitch. That is not to say that these good producers will not be advertised! Their owners are very proud of their accomplishments and will advertise them to be available to approved bitches and to reputable breeders who are breeding for the right reasons.

Owning a stud dog is no small job. The actual breeding process is not always simple. A stud dog must be kept in optimum condition and must be trained in the right breeding habits. One must have the facilities to accommodate the visiting bitches and the time to invest in the actual breedings. Also, if bitches are accepted for breeding, they may be hard to breed, resulting in a visit to the veterinarian for possible artificial insemination.

When your stud dog is used, you must be prepared for half of the joy or half of the blame—or, in some cases, all of the blame. If the puppies are not what the breeder expected, you can bet it will be the stud dog's fault. If they are all beautiful and

Puppies can start to hear at about 10 days of age, and they will usually open their eyes at about 14 days of age. (Photo by Julie Phillips)

perfect, they will look just like their mother! Although this sounds humorous, it can be a source of frustration, and you should be prepared for it as a stud dog owner.

Think twice before offering your dog at stud. Does he have the desirable qualities called for in the Maltese standard? Would breeding to him enhance someone else's breeding program? Can you manage the time it takes to make sure the breedings are accomplished? If all the answers to these questions are yes and you decide to go ahead and offer your dog at stud, make sure he is mated only to bitches of good quality that are owned by very reputable breeders.

Care of Your Maltese Bitch in Whelp

The gestation period for a dog is sixty-three days. Puppies born much earlier than fifty-six days usually are not likely to survive. It is not unheard of for a Maltese to only carry her puppies to sixty-one or sixty-two days, and they will look just fine when born. But if your Maltese bitch has not whelped by the sixty-third day, keep a close watch on her. The conception may not have taken place on the actual day of the breeding, as the sperm can live to fertilize an egg for at least forty-eight hours. If she shows any unusual signs of discharge or distress, contact the veterinarian.

You should keep your bitch on her normal amount of food and exercise for the first four weeks of her pregnancy. You may not even be able to notice that she is pregnant unless she has had morning sickness or has gone off her food. She

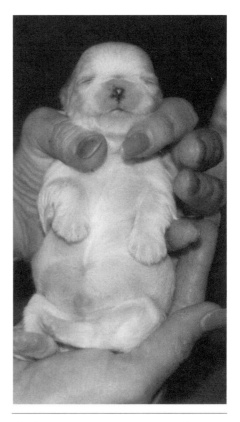

Maltese puppies are very tiny and can weigh as little as 2 or 3 ounces at birth. This little one is about a week old. (Photo by Suzanne Johnston)

will begin to need more food as the fifth week approaches and will probably accept it heartily. Her diet should be high in calories and protein at this time. Cottage cheese added to one meal can be very appetizing. Do not add a multitude of new vitamins to her food because this could cause an imbalance.

If you feed your bitch a good, nutritious food like the ones listed in Chapter 7 and a good supplement (such as Missing Link), she should have an adequate diet. I usually increase the feedings at this time from two to three per day, and you should give the bitch only a mild amount of exercise. As she gets increasingly bigger, she may require more rest in between bouts of play. Adequate exercise is necessary during pregnancy to keep the muscles in good shape for whelping. When she has reached the seventh week, make sure she is handled with care and is not allowed to jump or play roughly.

Your bitch will probably become much more affectionate during her pregnancy and will want a lot of attention from you. As she approaches her due date, spend more time with her daily and make sure her hair is trimmed in such a way that it will not interfere with the whelping or nursing of the puppies. At this time, call your veterinarian and find out if he will be on call or available for you at the time the puppies are due.

We usually start taking the bitch's temperature three times a day starting with the fifty-sixth to fifty-eighth day. This will give you an idea of when it starts to change. Normally, the temperature will gradually decrease as the time for the puppies approaches. It will rise each evening. When it drops a full degree or goes to 99°F or below, your bitch will whelp within twenty-four hours. If she does not, there may be a problem, and you need to contact your veterinarian. Keeping this record is important because a bitch usually will follow the same type pattern of temperatures on her succeeding litters, and this information can be helpful.

Whelping the Puppies

The following supplies are needed for delivering the puppies:

- Small towels or wash rags to rub the puppies

- Small sterile scissors for cutting the umbilical cord

- Small forceps for clamping the umbilical cord

- Alcohol for sterilizing the instruments

- Hot water bottles to keep the puppies warm

- Iodine to put on the umbilical cord

- Dental floss to tie off the umbilical cord

- An infrared lamp to put above the whelping box

When your bitch goes into labor, her temperature will rise, and she will begin scratching around in her box or pen, trying to nest. She may shake or pant. You can tell if she is having contractions by watching her abdomen. It could take several hours from the start of the nesting to the time when she really gets down to hard contractions. If your bitch has labored for an hour and has not produced a puppy, it may be time for you to call the veterinarian. Don't wait until your bitch is exhausted to do this. There may be any number of reasons why a Maltese will need a cesarean section. The first puppy may be blocking the others if he is large or is being born breech or feet first. The bitch may get overly tired and stop contractions all together. Whatever the reason, it is important that you act

Be prepared ahead of time for the delivery of the puppies and the care of the dam and her litter in the critical days that follow. Dolly looks like a very satisfied mother! (Photo by Larry Abbott)

Unclamp the forceps and cut the cord with a sterile scissors. Dab iodine on the cord where it was cut. Continue to rub the puppy lightly with a dry wash rag and keep him warm. If you need to give your attention to another puppy being born, you can place the first puppy next to the hot water bottle to keep him warm until you can get back to him. Once all the puppies have arrived and are breathing nicely, you can put them on the mother and see if you can encourage them to nurse. Ann Seranne, in her book *The Joy of Breeding Your Own Show Dog,* offers a much more detailed explanation of how to breed and whelp dogs,

quickly to save the lives of your bitch and the puppies. If your veterinarian has been notified ahead of time, he may suggest that you meet him at the clinic. You will need one person to drive and one person to watch the bitch because car movement has been known to make contractions increase, and many puppies have been born on the way to the vet!

Whether born naturally or by cesarean section, the process after the puppy is out is the same. Break the sac at the nose of the puppy and wipe out his mouth, leaving the cord and placenta attached for the time being. Get the puppy breathing and then clamp the cord with a small forceps about an inch from the puppy's body. Take a 6-inch piece of dental floss and tie the cord tightly (knotting the floss) right above the forceps.

Weigh the puppies every day for the first few days and then weekly thereafter. They should continue to grow and gain weight. Failure to do so can indicate a problem. (Photo by Elsie Burke)

especially the Toy breeds. It is a must for the Toy dog breeder. In her book, she stresses that energy is what a puppy needs most in the first twenty-four to forty-eight hours until the bitch's milk can fully come down. She does not encourage supplementing until after this time, and she provides a recipe for glucose drops to give to the puppies to save them and give them energy to nurse. We strongly recommend this procedure because it has worked for us for years, and we use Ann's glucose drop recipe to this day.

Raising Puppies

For the first five to six weeks, your bitch will take care of feeding and cleaning the puppies while you take care of feeding and cleaning her. You will need to keep the room warm, and for about the first week or so, the infrared lamp will need to be positioned so it warms one corner of the box that the bitch and the puppies are in. The puppies or dam can then move to the cooler side of the box if it gets too warm. We usually attach the lamp so it is positioned above the puppies about four or five feet and is situated where it could not possibly fall into the box.

   We do not recommend heating pads because they can burn the bitch or the puppies. We have also been warned by veterinarians that the pads can make the blood pool in a puppy's body.

   Once the puppies are about 5 or 6 weeks old, it will be time to start weaning them.

   When beginning to wean your puppies, wait until they have not eaten for a while. You can remove the bitch and let her have some free time

Begin weaning your puppies by putting their food into a wide, shallow dish. Soon most of the food will be going into their mouths and not all over the place! (Photo by Julie Phillips)

for an hour or so and then introduce the puppies to their first solid food. We usually grind up a good dry puppy food (such as Precise Growth) into a powder. To that we add enough goat's milk formula to make an oatmeal consistency. Concentrated goat's milk comes in a can in the grocery store and can be diluted with distilled water, three cans of water to one can of goat's milk. *Do not use cow's milk on puppies.* Only use the goat's milk or formula created especially for puppies (such as Just Born or Esbilac) that you can find in the pet store. Place the mixture in a shallow dish and into the pen with the puppies. If they do not seem to want to investigate, you can gently stick their noses into the food, and they will have to lick it off their face. They will soon be very happy to see you put that dish in the pen! Do this two to three times a day, placing the bitch back in with them after they are finished. Soon, when they seem to be getting enough food during the day from the dish, you can take the bitch out all day and only return her at night. Maltese puppies will usually be totally weaned at about 6 or 7 weeks of age, depending on how long the breeder wants to keep them with the dam.

It also may depend on how long the dam wants to put up with them, especially after their little teeth start to come in. It is good for the puppies to have the social interaction with their mother and their siblings. Most Maltese mothers love their puppies immensely and will play with them and teach them when they get too rough.

A conscientious breeder continually strives to produce better and better quality puppies and hopes for the litter that will produce that Best in Show winner! (Photo by Larry & Vicki Abbott)

MORE THAN JUST ONE?

If you have read this entire chapter, it must be evident to you by now how much education, work and dedication go into producing quality Maltese. If you are not inclined to undertake this giant responsibility, you can at least appreciate all the work it took to produce your lovely companion animal! The dedicated Maltese breeder will most likely not be satisfied with producing only an occasional good dog here or there; he will have a goal of improving the quality, step-by-step, of all the dogs in his kennel. The satisfaction derived from accomplishing this is what keeps most good breeders involved over a long period of time. And, by the way, you don't have to be a breeder to own more than one Maltese!

You don't have to be a breeder to have more than one Maltese in your family! (Photo by Julie Phillips)

(photo by Pamela Rightmyer & Furrari Photography)

CHAPTER THIRTEEN

Special Care for Your Older Maltese

How fast a dog ages is individual to the particular dog, his activity level and his health. Fortunately for us, toy breeds tend to age less rapidly than the larger breeds. While a Great Dane or a German Shepherd may reach old age at 10 to 12 years old, a Maltese will not be old until he is between 14 and 16 years old. When a dog becomes sick or is injured, the aging process can be accelerated. The care of your older Maltese should be aimed at preventing his premature aging as much as possible through good nutrition, regular visits to the veterinarian and keeping a watchful eye for any unusual problems that may surface. Physical stress is not the only type of stress that will contribute to aging. Dogs can be mentally stressed as well, which can cause sleeplessness or anxiety, which in turn puts physical stress on the dog's body. Watching for the signs that your dog may need treatment or a special kind of care will help lengthen his life considerably.

SIGNS OF AGING

When your dog starts to become old, you may notice that he becomes less energetic and does not engage in as much activity as he used to. This may happen so gradually that you will not notice it

Your older Maltese may slow down and want to spend more time sleeping during the day than he used to. (Photo by Larry & Vicki Abbott)

immediately. He may begin to sleep longer during the day or begin to get short of breath when you take your walks. He may not be as curious about new things or be less willing to play the games you are used to seeing him participate in. He is gradually slowing down. This may or may not be the case for your dog. Some Maltese will have a great active time until they die suddenly or become ill. If your Maltese seems to be slowing down, you will need to take him to the veterinarian for a good checkup to make sure something besides aging is not the cause of the symptoms you are seeing.

As they age, Maltese can start to lose the dark pigment that was once on their nose and around their eye rims. It may turn to brown or may go altogether pink. Their skin may start to become dry or scaly and flake or become itchy as a result of reduced activity of the oil glands. Sometimes you will find little skin tumors, or warts, which are common. Your dog's toe pads may become cracked and dry, and his nails will need to be clipped more often.

Older dogs have less tolerance for change. They do not care for upsets in their daily routine and will get stressed if this happens. Boarding an older dog while you are away is not a good idea because he will become irritable and anxious and may become ill as a result. His immune system is also not as good as it once was, so exposing him to a lot of different dogs at this time would not be advisable. If at all possible, find someone to care for your older dog at home if you must be away. This will be much less stressful for him and less worrisome for you.

Loss of hearing is common in old age, and you may find that your dog does not respond to you the way he once did. If the hearing loss is gradual, the dog will adapt to it and will not really know the difference. This could be dangerous for the dog if you were to let him loose outside and then try to call him to keep him from harm. You can test his hearing by clapping behind his back to see if he responds. If you do it within his sight range, he may be responding to the movement, which he will have adapted to do.

An older dog is more prone to tooth and gum decay, and you may start to notice that this is progressing more rapidly. Older dogs need the same dental care that your younger puppy did. If you keep up the good dental practices all of your dog's life, you will have fewer problems when he ages. It is normal for an older dog, especially a Toy, to lose teeth as he ages, and removal of a bad tooth may actually improve his health. Later in life, a gray or blue haze may come over your dog's eyes due to the aging of the lens. This can be mistaken for cataracts, which can also occur in old age. The best way to tell what is really happening to your dog's eyes is to have them checked by your veterinarian. The haze, if not a cataract, will not affect your dog's vision greatly.

A nice warm pillow or bed is important as your dog gets older. Joints can get stiff from sleeping on cold or damp flooring. (Photo by Julie Phillips)

Your dog may develop arthritis in parts of his body and may start to limp or hobble along. This can be due to an old injury or bone disease, or he may just be stiff from sleeping in a drafty, cold or damp area. Giving your dog a warm, soft place to sleep is very important as he ages.

How to Care for These Changes

Your older Maltese may need more frequent veterinary checkups. A well-cared-for pet will live a longer life. After your Maltese is 6 or 7 years old, he should probably see a veterinarian about every six months to have his blood tested and his stool and urine checked. This can assist in early detection of any symptoms of kidney or liver failure or deterioration. The vet will check for cataracts, conditions such as heart disease and any breakdown of the dog's immune system. Some problems, such as cataracts, can easily be corrected by surgery and would enhance the dog's life.

Kidneys

An older dog that has kidney problems will probably have accidents in the house. There are special diets to help correct this problem before your dog goes into kidney failure. If your dog seems to be drinking an unusual amount of water, he may have a kidney problem. Do not lessen his water intake at this time. Water should be available at all times for your older dog, especially if you suspect kidney dysfunction. If you have a bitch that has a problem with accidents, it could be because of a decrease in estrogen. Some older spayed bitches develop this condition, and it can be easily treated with doses of estrogen.

Constipation

This can be caused by improper diet and/or a weakening of the muscles in the abdominal wall with age. Constipation can sometimes be caused by enlargement of the prostate in the male dog. Check with your veterinarian about a diet for your older dog that's good for his bowel activity.

Make sure his anal glands are expressed so they do not become impacted. If you see blood in your dog's stool at any time, it is a wise idea to have him checked by your veterinarian. Older dogs can be prone to irritable bowel syndrome, which can lead to other problems. Blood can also be an indication of a condition in the colon that may need attention.

Heart Disease or Stroke

Signs of heart disease may be difficult to detect in the early stages. If your dog seems listless, has shortness of breath or has developed a soft continuous cough, suspect a heart problem. If your dog is also over-weight, this can compli-cate the matter. On the other hand, if you never notice anything and then one day your older dog has trouble getting up or seems dazed or confused, he may have suffered a mild stroke. Your veterinarian should be contacted for any of these problems. There are heart medications you can give your dog to alleviate the symptoms and make him more comfortable.

Muscles and Joints

With age comes loss of muscle tone and stiffness of the joints due to bones aging. Care must be taken to keep your dog from sleeping in drafty areas or on cold or damp floors. Osteoarthritis can set in, making it difficult for your dog to move. Moderate exercise can continue to help the muscles and joints move more freely. Your veteri-narian may prescribe aspirin or some other form of pain reliever for arthritis of the joints. Never give your dog Tylenol or any other product without consult-ing your vet. These drugs can be lethal to dogs.

Deafness

With an older dog, there may be loss of hearing. Unfortunately, there is no cure for the gradual

Your older dog should have regular checkups by your vet-erinarian on a more frequent basis than when he was a puppy. (Photo by M. Martin)

loss of hearing due to old age. Take your dog to the veterinarian if you suspect he is losing his hearing. This could be caused by something other than old age such as something blocking the ear canal, in which case it might be treatable.

Cataracts

Your older dog may develop cataracts. If your dog is having difficulty getting around, he may need to have the cataracts removed. When you notice a change in the color of your dog's eyes, check with your veterinarian. Your dog may just have a gray or blue haze on his eye due to the aging process of the lens, and it may not be cataracts.

Keeping up with your dog's dental needs can make his senior years more comfortable. Infected teeth and gums can cause disease and deteriorate his health. (Photo by Pegini Photography)

Teeth and Gums

As your Maltese gets older, he will have more and more tooth and gum problems. Toy dogs are especially prone to bad tooth decay and can lose teeth very early in their lives. Tooth decay can lead to a very sick dog because the infection from the teeth or gums can locate elsewhere in the dog's body. This can even cause death. When your dog gets older, his immune system is not as up to fighting these infections as it once was. Removal of some teeth may be necessary to maintain your dog's overall health. Make sure you check your dog's teeth often and have them cleaned by your veterinarian if he recommends it. Blood testing may need to be done before your older dog is administered an anesthetic to avoid any problems during surgery. Usually it is not a wise idea to administer anesthetic to a dog that is compromised by illness or organ deficiencies. Continue your program of dental hygiene all throughout your dog's life, even into old age.

GOOD NUTRITION FOR YOUR OLDER MALTESE

As your Maltese gets older, he will probably become less active, therefore requiring less food and calories per day than when he was a younger, more active dog. Most owners do not realize this until the dog starts to become obese, causing stress on his heart and other organs and shortening his life. The food you feed your Maltese during this time in his life needs to be of the same high quality as you have always fed him, only with less fat and calories. There are many good dog foods today that are made especially for the older dog. Most of the brands mentioned in Chapter 7 (such as Innova, Flint River Ranch, Precise, and Wyssong) have special foods for seniors that are balanced for their needs.

If blood tests on your dog have determined that a special diet is needed for a particular problem such as liver dysfunction, kidney stones, allergies and so on, there are foods available that are designed for the treatment of that particular problem. If your veterinarian prescribes one of these special diets, you must make sure your dog stays on it and does not receive extra treats or snacks. Giving any older dog lots of table scraps or treats between meals will only add to the imbalance of his diet and lead to obesity. Eliminate bones or bone chips from an older dog's diet as well as very dry biscuits, as they can lead to bowel obstructions and make the stool very hard.

An older dog should be kept on a schedule. He will look forward to his meals coming at the same time in the morning and evening each day. Changing this drastically could cause stress and create bowel problems. If your older dog goes off his food for more than a day, it is a wise idea to have him checked by your veterinarian. Make sure he does not get dehydrated. If he will not drink, you can give him water by filling a syringe (with the needle removed) and then squirting the water into his mouth. Sometimes an electrolyte mixture such as *Pedialyte,* sold in the infant department at the grocery store, can be good for restoring your older dog's energy. Check with your veterinarian

As your dog ages, he may become more sensitive to fleas or become allergic to things he never used to have a problem with because of the change in his immune system. Keep an eye out for any symptoms that might necessitate some action on your part. (Photo by Jennifer Neis)

before administering anything besides water to your dog.

GROOMING YOUR OLDER MALTESE

Your Maltese will develop different needs in grooming as he ages. The skin of an older dog will become drier, and he will mat more easily. The oil-producing glands will not be as active, and his skin may need to be treated with a special moisturizer. A little oil can be added to the final rinse in his bath if the problem is very bad. Realize, however, that this will also leave the hair a little oily, but it may be necessary to alleviate the skin problem. Check to make sure the skin problem on your Maltese is not a thyroid deficiency, as this can be easily treated with a small pill given every day.

Sometimes an older dog's immune system will begin to break down, and you'll see things that his system suppressed as a younger dog. Demodectic mange is one of those things that can crop up on a dog that is stressed or that has a compromised immune system. The demodex mites, which have been kept under control all this time, will surface and cause hair loss in patches, redness and scaling of the skin and intense itching. See your veterinarian if you notice any of these symptoms; it is necessary to treat this type of mite with a special medication such as Goodwinol or Canex. He will do skin scrapings and then examine them under a microscope to evaluate whether this problem is demodectic mange.

Sometimes frequent changes in medications will help eliminate the problem faster. If the sores are not mange, they may turn out to be hot spots. Hot spots are patches of skin where the hair has been lost; they will be red and irritated and even sometimes extremely infected with pus. This is a bacterial infection that will drive your dog nuts trying to lick or scratch it. For an older dog, it can be a severe stress and must be treated immediately. Clip away any hair that is still attached and wash the affected area with an antibiotic soap. There are topical treatments, such as Sulfadene, that you can purchase at a pet store, and they should help alleviate this problem. Your veterinarian may prescribe oral antibiotics to aid in your dog's recovery.

It may be advantageous as your Maltese gets older to trim his hair shorter to make him more comfortable. Getting huge mats out of an older dog can be painful for him because his skin will be thinner and more sensitive at this time of his life. You can actually cause redness, rashes and even infection by opening up the pores and irritating the skin. The nose of the dog and the pads of the feet may become dry and cracked. Vaseline or hypoallergenic lotion can be applied to these areas to alleviate this condition.

The toenails on an older dog will grow at a faster rate, so you will probably need to trim your dog's toenails more often.

Clipping the hair short can be more comfortable for your older dog. (Photo by Lynda Podgurski)

Fresh air, sunshine and exercise are still essential to the health and well-being of your Maltese, even as he ages. If he will not self-exercise much any more, you can take him on very brief walks to strengthen his heart and lungs. (Photo by Julie Phillips)

Care must be taken when bathing the dog so he does not slip and cause damage to his joints. Wrap him in a warm towel after bathing, and dry him immediately so he does not get chilled. This can stiffen his joints and lead to arthritis.

EXERCISE FOR THE OLDER DOG

It has been said by many breeders that Maltese will act like perpetual puppies even into old age. This is very true unless the dog is suffering from an ailment or is extremely obese. There are dogs that are self-motivated and dogs that are lazy. You know what your dog's normal activity level has been all along, and though he will slow down somewhat as he ages, he should still receive regular exercise to keep his muscles, joints and heart in the best working order possible for his age. You can still walk with your older dog, and it will be good for him. You may need to slow the pace down or shorten the walks, however, so you don't go beyond what your older dog is capable of enduring and create undue stress on his body.

SENIORITY AND THE NEW PUPPY

At some time as your Maltese gets older, you may consider adding a new puppy to the household. This can be very stressful but very rewarding in the long run to your older dog. Care must be taken to respect the older dog's position in the family, as well as his belongings and his space, so he does not feel threatened.

Companionship of other dogs as your dog ages can encourage him to be more active and consequently improve his health and well-being. Care must be taken not to stress an older dog when he is adjusting to a new member of the family. (Photo by Julie Phillips)

When introducing the new puppy to your older dog, make sure it is not in a place where the older dog feels his territory is being challenged. A neutral area, such as the breeder's home where you are purchasing the puppy or even a relative's home, can be a good choice. Hold the new puppy in your lap and let the older dog come to you. This is a safer and more subtle approach than just letting the puppy loose when you walk in the door. A new bouncy puppy may be an irritation at first, but usually the older Maltese will accept him and may try to ignore him. As the puppy gets older, your older dog may start to view this other dog as more of a playmate. This can add years to your older dog's life because it will probably make him more active.

Avoid leaving the two dogs alone until the puppy is older because it could be dangerous for the younger dog. Make sure the puppy has his own area in your house that was not the older dog's place before. The puppy will need his own eating and sleeping area away from your other Maltese. An older dog can become very irritated if a puppy tries to take anything he is eating or chewing on, and he may snap at the puppy or hurt him.

Above all, be patient with the process of your older dog's acceptance of the puppy. Give both of them equal attention, and make sure your older dog knows he is not being replaced.

QUALITY OF LIFE

When your dog gets old, he may become ill or disabled because of a disease or condition that will not get any better. Some dogs can be made quite comfortable with extra care and medication. You may choose to let your dog live out his life comfortably and die in his own surroundings. This may involve hand-feeding your pet or carrying him out to relieve himself if he is not able to do this on his own.

There are some situations, however, in which the dog is suffering and will only get progressively worse. It is at that time that the owner may be faced with the prospect of having to put the dog to sleep. Although we would like to keep our beloved pets around for our own emotional needs, the truth is that some do not get any better and will suffer for a very long time. It is at this point that a decision must be made about what is best for your dog and the quality of life he is leading.

Not to leave the girls out, Ch. Sumtymes Miss Glory was the winner of the Veteran Bitch Class, and she also won an Award of Merit at the 1998 AMA National Specialty. This was quite an accomplishment and quite a beautiful performance, as she was almost 12 years old! Miss Glory is owned and handled by Jerry Lea McConnell.

During this time, your veterinarian may talk with you about the possibility of euthanasia. Euthanasia is the method by which a veterinarian can put your dog to sleep quickly and painlessly. It is not an easy choice, and it is one that must be made on an individual basis, considering all the options.

The Older Maltese—Your Constant Companion

When your Maltese was young, there weren't enough things to keep him occupied. His attention span was limited to say the least, and he was all over the place having a good time—with or without you. As your dog ages, he will want to spend more time just relaxing with you and staying close. His curiosity for new things will not be as dramatic as a puppy's can be. It is for this very reason that a lot of people would rather obtain an older dog for a companion than a very young puppy.

An older dog is more settled, and the relationship with him can be very rewarding. If you are interested in an older Maltese, contact the same reputable breeder that you would contact for a

Three generations of ladies at Louan's! (Photo by Elsie Burke)

puppy. They sometimes have very good quality dogs of differing ages that they'd be agreeable to placing in a loving home. Rescue organizations are also a good place to look for an older dog that may be in need of a very good home and special care. The American Maltese Association Rescue contacts can be found on their Web site at www.americanmaltese.org.

(Photo by Vicki Abbott)

CHAPTER FOURTEEN

The American Maltese Association

The national breed club is extremely important to the improvement and protection of the purebred dog. It is a collection of people with a common cause. Activities are organized to achieve goals concerning ethics in breeding practices, pertinent health issues and education. The American Maltese Association has, for some thirty-eight years, been active in achieving these goals for the Maltese breed.

HISTORY LEADING TO THE ORGANIZATION OF THE AMA

The very first standard for the Maltese breed in this country was established in 1906 through the efforts of Mr. and Mrs. Koerlin, who were instrumental in organizing the first Maltese Specialty club. This club was called the Maltese Terrier Club of America. The following is the original standard for Maltese:

Original Maltese Official Standard

GENERAL APPEARANCE   Intelligent, sprightly, affectionate, with long straight coat hanging evenly down each side, the parting extending from nose to root of tail. Although the frame is hidden beneath a mantle of hair, the general appearance should suggest a vigorous well proportioned body.

Three charter members of the American Maltese Association at the AMA Specialty in 1999—Florence Hopple, Marjorie Lewis and Larry Ward. (Photo by Vicki Abbott)

WEIGHT   Not to exceed 7 pounds. The smaller the better. Under three pounds ideal.

COLOR   Pure white.

COAT   Long, straight, silky and strong and of even texture throughout. No undercoat.

HEAD   In proportion to the size of the dog—should be of fair length; the skull slightly round, rather broad between the ears and moderately well defined at the temples: i.e., exhibiting a moderate amount of stop and not in one straight line from nose to occiput bone.

MUZZLE   Not lean or snipy, but delicately proportioned.

NOSE   Black.

EARS   Drop ears set slightly low, profusely covered with long hair.

EYES   Very dark—not too far apart—expression alert but gentle; black eye rims give a more beautiful expression.

LEGS   Short, straight, fine boned and well feathered.

FEET   Small with long feathering.

BODY AND SHAPE   Back short and level. Body low to ground, deep loins.

TAIL AND CARRIAGE   Tail well feathered with long hair, gracefully carried, its end resting on the hindquarters and side.

Scale of Positive Points

Weight and size	20
Coat	20
Color	10
Body and shape	10
Tail and its carriage	10
Head	10
Eyes	5
Legs	5
Feet	5
Nose	5
Total	**100**

Scale of Negative Points

Hair clipped from face or feet	20
Kinky, curly or outstanding coat	15
Uneven texture of coat	10
Yellow or any color on ears or coat	10
Undershot or overshot jaw	10
Prominent or bulging eyes	10
Pig nose or deep stop	10
Roach back	5
Legginess	5
Butterfly or dudley nose	5
Total	**100**

Aennchen Antonelli, seen here with one of her Group-winning Maltese, was one of the early officers of the American Maltese Association.(Photo courtesy of Larry Ward & Frank Oberstar)

As you can see, this early standard differs in places from the current AKC standard, especially when it refers to size. The preferred size now is 4 to 6 pounds.

Over the years, the club formed by the Koerlins became the National Maltese Club, which held its first Specialty in 1917. The interest in the Maltese breed and clubs grew; by the 1950s, there were two organizations. The National Maltese Club had become the Maltese Dog Club of America, and a second new club was formed, the Maltese Dog Fanciers of America. Dr. Calvaresi (Villa Malta), who was mentioned in the historical chapters, and a group of Maltese fanciers who mostly owned his breeding were active in the Maltese Dog Club of America. Mrs. Virginia Leitch and the Antonellis, also aforementioned, were involved in the Maltese Dog Fanciers of America.

When the time came to hold a National Specialty Show, the American Kennel Club would not approve one without the sanctioning of one parent club for the breed. It was at this time, in 1961, when the two clubs came together to meet in New York City to form the American Maltese Association.

The first officers of the AMA were Dr. Calvaresi, President; Helen Schively Poggi, Vice President West; Aennchen Antonelli, Vice President East; and Tony Antonelli, Secretary-Treasurer. The list read like a Who's Who of Maltese in the United States! This newly formed American Maltese Association had its first meeting in

An award table at the American Maltese Association National Specialty. (Photo by Vicki Abbott)

Herbert Kellogg, 1967–69
Gini Sumner Evans, 1970–71
Larry Ward, 1972–74
Joanne Hess, 1975
Anna Mae Hardy, 1976
Robert Bergquist, 1977–78
Anna Mae Hardy, 1979–80
Stephen G. Feldblum, 1981–82
Nicholas Cutillo, 1983–84
Marge Rozik, 1985–86
Dorothy White, 1987–88
Kathy Blackard, 1989
Robert Bergquist, 1990–97
Larry Abbott, 1998–2000

New York in 1963 in conjunction with the Westminster Kennel Club. One of the first projects they undertook was to put together and submit a new Maltese standard. This was sent to the American Kennel Club for approval and started being used in 1964.

From this very small beginning, the American Maltese Association has grown to be the most important leader in this country concerning the Maltese breed. As the parent club, the responsibility is great as the breed continues to be more and more popular.

Presidents of the American Maltese Association

Dr. Vincenzo Calvaresi, 1961–62
Dr. Helen Schively Poggi, 1963
Anne Pendleton, 1964–66

Early American Maltese Association Shows

The first B match held by the newly formed American Maltese Association was in July 1963 in Pasadena, California. The judge for this match was

A typical class at an AMA National Specialty. (Photo by Vicki Abbott)

Bob Craig, husband of Eloise Craig, who became one of the organization's hardest workers. She served in several capacities as secretary, vice president and treasurer for eight years. She also was the editor of the newsletter, the *Maltese Rx,* from the early 1960s until her death in 1983. The second B match for the club was held in Santa Ana, California. Ann Pendleton judged this match, and she, too, was an important worker for the early AMA. She served as president for three successive years and was instrumental in getting the AMA Specialty shows recognized by the American Kennel Club.

The first A match was held in Louisville, Ohio, on June 28, 1964, at the home of Ann and Stewart Pendleton. Multiple breed judge Maxwell Riddle officiated at the match and chose Edward's Wee Holly as his winner. There was also an obedience competition at this first A match. Ch. Scipio of Villa Malta was the obedience winner. The second A match for the AMA was also held at the Pendleton home in 1964. Handler Wynn Suck judged this match, which also included an obedience competition. Sun Canyon Matinee Idol was the match winner, and Ch. Good Time Terry Lynn won the obedience competition. This little obedience dog was trained by Herb Kellogg.

June 11, 1966, was a day of celebration for all Maltese fanciers in the United States because it was the first American Maltese Association National Specialty. Held in Ohio in conjunction with the Columbiana Kennel Club show, it was well attended with more than fifty Maltese entered. Mr. William Kendrick officiated and chose Ch. Co-Ca-He's Aennchen's Toy Dancer as the winner; this dog went on to place second in the Toy Group that day. Toy became very famous, being the first Maltese to ever win a Toy Group at Westminster Kennel Club.

The most recent winner of the AMA National Specialty (1999) was Ch. Showboat Miss Piggy of C and M, owned by Barbara Brown and Peter J. Rogers III. (Photo by Vicki Abbott)

Since this first AMA National Specialty in 1966, the American Maltese Association has held a National Specialty every year on a rotating basis between the East, Midwest and West. In the year 2000, the group will celebrate its 35th National Specialty in Las Vegas, Nevada.

For the Protection of the Breed

Within the American Maltese Association are committees that are constantly at work for the protection of the Maltese breed. Three of these very important committees are the AMA Rescue

Committee, the AMA Education Committee and the AMA Health and Welfare Committee. Having been the recording secretary of the American Maltese Association for seventeen years (1981–98), I have been privileged to watch the continued dedication of many committees within the club over a period of time. These volunteers have given many hours of their lives for the love of the Maltese breed.

The American Maltese Association is a group of individuals with a common purpose—the welfare and protection of the Maltese. (Photo by Crisandra Maltese)

The AMA Rescue Committee is, unfortunately, probably one of the busiest committees in the American Maltese Association. These extremely dedicated volunteer members receive countless phone calls from individuals knowing of Maltese

that need to be rescued. Some, if not most, of these needy Maltese require medical attention that can be quite costly. Funds are raised through the AMA to keep this project going for the benefit of the breed.

Three AMA members were instrumental in founding and implementing the AMA Rescue program: Ann Glenn, Debra Kirsch and Beverly Passe. The Rescue areas are divided into East, Midwest and West. To contact one of the current AMA Rescue Chairmen, either retrieve the information from the AMA Web site or contact the current corresponding secretary with the information provided to you by the American Kennel Club.

The Education Committee is dedicated to the improvement of the Maltese breed through knowledge. The committee is comprised of a group of very experienced breeders who are willing to give of their time to be mentors and educators. At the National Specialty every year, seminars on various subjects are offered for anyone who wants to attend. Recently, the committee was proud to announce the completion of *The Illustrated Guide to the Maltese,* which took many years to finish. The AMA Education committee members whose input was invaluable in the production of this guide were Mary Day, Lynda Podgurski, Jeanne Hess, Glynette Cass, Carol Neth, Dottie White, Ann Glenn, Pam Armstrong and myself. Combined, it

of the Maltese breed. It is the hope of this committee that, through knowledge and a more informed understanding of the Maltese Breed Standard, there will be better breeders and judges and, consequently, better Maltese.

In addition to *The Illustrated Guide to the Maltese*, a very good video is available about the standard. In the 1980s, a separate AMA committee comprised of myself, Daryl Martin and Susan Sandlin worked to produce this Maltese video that is now sold by the American Kennel Club. The video adds to the information in the written booklet, providing a realistic view of the Maltese in action that cannot be obtained just through pictures alone.

The AMA is committed to the education of breeders and judges for the continual improvement of the breed. (Photo by Margaret D. Lewis & Robert Goldman)

Catherine Lawrence has been instrumental in setting up the AMA Donor Advised Fund for Maltese through the AKC Canine Health Foundation. Through raffles, such as this one at the 1999 AMA Specialty, money is raised for the health and welfare of the breed. (Photo by Vicki Abbott)

was unbelievable the number of years of experience in the breed this committee represented. This guide is now used in Breed Standard seminars offered around the country for breeders and judges

The AMA Health and Welfare Committee is charged with the protection of the health of the Maltese. This committee is active in raising funds to contribute to particular research projects. These projects are dedicated to finding cures for disease and conditions affecting the Maltese and possibly other toy breeds. Most recently—with the persistence of committee members Catherine Lawrence and Cynthia Smith, DVM—the AMA Health and Welfare Committee set up an AMA Donor Advised Fund within the American Kennel Club Canine Health Foundation. AMA members or any Maltese fancier can contribute to this research directly through the designated fund. To find out how to become a part of the health and welfare of the breed, contact the committee chairman on the AMA Web site or contact the AKC Canine Health Foundation and ask about the specific AMA Donor Advised Fund.

The American Maltese Association Breeder Referral

The American Maltese Association is available to help any person interested in more information about the Maltese breed. A Breeder Referral Contact will send out a packet of information concerning the breed and will include in this packet a list of AMA breeders from around the country. This is the best place to start your search for a puppy because these members will know other reputable breeders in their areas and can be very helpful in sending you in the right direction, even if they do not have puppies at the moment. The AMA is concerned about the welfare of

Maltese and is dedicated to helping prospective owners become as informed as possible. To locate the AMA Breeder Referral Contact, check on the AMA Web site for the current person holding this position or call the American Kennel Club and ask for the AMA Breeder Referral Contact.

The Maltese Rx

The Maltese Rx is the newsletter publication of the American Maltese Association. This newsletter has been the primary communication from the club to its members and subscribers for almost forty years. *The Maltese Rx* contains club business, news about Maltese, articles and pictures from around the country and even overseas. It is published eleven times a year, and anyone interested in the Maltese breed can subscribe. Check the AMA Web site for how to subscribe if you are interested or contact the current *Maltese Rx* editor. (This information can be obtained from the current AMA corresponding secretary provided to you by the American Kennel Club.)

Special Awards Given by the American Maltese Association

Each year at the awards banquet held after the judging of the National Specialty, the AMA presents awards for achievements by AMA members and their Maltese. The awards are for the Top Winning Maltese, the Top Owner-Handled Maltese, the Top Producing Maltese (sire and dam), the Top Breeders and Co-Breeders, the Top Obedience Maltese and the Top Junior Showmanship Winner for Maltese.

The Carol Frances Andersen Breeder's Award is given to the breeder of the Top Maltese each year in memory of Top Maltese Breeder Carol Frances Andersen. (Photo by Vicki Abbott)

Jerry Lea McConnell receives an award from the American Maltese Association for her Top Owner-Handled Maltese. (Photo by Vicki Abbott)

In addition, the Carol Frances Andersen Breeder's Award is given to the breeder of the Top Maltese by Larry and Vicki Abbott in memory of

Carol Frances Andersen, the breeder of the top winning Maltese Dog of all time.

At the banquet, AMA Outstanding Members are recognized, and the Sunshine Frost Awards are given for the Maltese Champions that have finished for the previous year. The Sunshine Frost Award is named for two very loved young Maltese fanciers who lost their lives much too soon.

A Challenge Trophy is given at the AMA National Specialty in memory of Frank Oberstar. (Photo by Henry Schley)

At the AMA Specialty, two trophies are given in memory of famous Maltese personalities. The Frank E. Oberstar Memorial Challenge Trophy is given for Best of Breed, and the Rena Martin Memorial Trophy is given for the Best Bred–By–Exhibitor Maltese.

The American Maltese Association presents a Best Bred-By-Exhibitor Trophy each year in memory of Rena Martin.

THE AMERICAN MALTESE ASSOCIATION CODE OF ETHICS

Although the complete AMA code of ethics appears in Appendix B, it must be noted here that the ethics of member breeders is of great importance to the American Maltese Association. Every AMA member must sign this code of ethics before being accepted into the organization. While the AMA is not a policing body, it expects the individual members to adhere to this code for the betterment of the breed and the club. AMA members are dedicated to controlling overpopulation and educating prospective Maltese owners in the responsibilities of ownership. As a result of this commitment, they will screen puppy buyers and people who want to breed to their dogs to make sure the Maltese breed is protected.

(*Photo by Taylor Taylor*)

Epilogue

The Maltese has long been admired and treasured for its beautiful white coat and gentle attitude. The size makes the breed a perfect, portable companion, and the dogs have great crowd appeal! Maltese have received public exposure since the very early days of time, but they have appeared more recently in the arms of dazzling personalities such as Elizabeth Taylor. They appear in movies, television advertisements and soap operas. Yet they seem to be undaunted by the whole thing, remaining as playful and loving as they always have been. This is a tribute to the Maltese breeders we have mentioned since the early 1900s, each generation of Maltese breeders has worked earnestly to keep the Maltese what it is today.

The appearance of the Maltese has changed somewhat over the years as breeders and exhibitors follow the trends toward the look of the dogs that are winning. Beauty is in the eye of the beholder, so to speak, and there is room in the standard for much opinion. One trend seems to last for awhile, and then another trend will come along. Throughout all this, the breeders dedicated to producing better and better dogs have maintained the quality of the breed for those that follow. The future is bright.

Much credit must be given to the owners and handlers who have improved grooming techniques for this breed, making the Maltese look lovelier and lovelier. It is a most breathtaking sight to watch a National Specialty and see the beautiful white dogs all lined up in a row. We've come a long way from sticking the dog in the sink, pouring cornstarch over it, and then trying to brush it out! There have been many advances made in products to care for Maltese coats, and they are looking wonderful.

When searching for your ideal puppy, realize that there is a wide variety of looks within the breed, as Maltese differ greatly in their size, coat and head structure. A 3-pound Maltese could be exhibited in the

The Maltese is a very popular breed, and it has received much public exposure through television, movies, greeting cards and advertisements. (Photo by Sandra Kenner & Christine Pearson)

as well as what he was gifted with hereditarily.

The popularity of this very famous breed has unfortunately been part of its downfall. Maltese puppies can bring fairly good prices, and there is the temptation by unscrupulous people to use the attractiveness of the Maltese as a moneymaker. Buyers can be enthralled by the striking appearance of the Maltese and not be aware of the responsibility that goes with owning a dog with such a luxurious coat. When the owner has not been properly educated in the care of the breed, the dog is usually the loser. When looking for a puppy to buy, resist the sales tactics used with the bargain puppy and go for the reputable breeder with years of experience. This story will have a happier ending.

same ring as a 7-pound Maltese, and they would both need to be considered for overall quality. Coats range from very dense and profuse to thinner and flatter. Differences in the structure of the head will end up creating a variety of expressions. They can all look different and yet all be good representatives of the breed.

Whatever look you are searching for, the temperament should always be the same—gentle, playful, loving and inquisitive.

A look from a Maltese should melt your heart. Reputable breeders who have made it their goal to produce this type of temperament should be the ones you seek out when looking for your companion. Remember that environment plays a big part in a puppy's personality after he is born

Look for correct Maltese temperament in the puppy you are searching for—he should be playful, loving and inquisitive. (Photo by Judy Crowe)

Unfortunately, the popularity of the Maltese has been part of its downfall. Always look for a puppy from a reputable breeder—one that is concerned about improvement of the breed.

We have seen through the ages how the Maltese has captured the hearts of men and women alike. The following poem, "A Fairy Tale," is an excerpt from the book *The Maltese Dog* by Virginia Leitch, originally printed in 1953. It is one of the most loved poems about this breed and has been passed down through the years. She placed it at the front of the book as an introduction to all the factual material to follow, but most Maltese fanciers will remember the poem better than anything else, even though the book contains close to 500 pages.

A FAIRY TALE

If you believe in fairy tales, and many people do,
I'll write one of the Maltese dog, and also one that's true.
The fairy tale will linger on about your Maltese pet,
While the truth that's writ about him, I'm sure you'll soon forget.

★　　★　　★　　★　　★　　★

Once 'pon a time, long, long ago, so it's been told to me,
There lived a beauteous maiden on an island in the sea.
The fairies called her Melita, *or* Melitae, *in fun*
But Issa *was her real name, which means* Thou Beautiful One.
Her eyes were black, like starless nights, yet hidden fires there shone
In opalescent colours, like diamonds, precious stones.
Her hair, like silver moonbeams, swept the ground on which she trod
O'er slippery rocks and jagged cliffs, and on the grassy sod.
She feared none of the big wild beasts that roamed the country side,
She seemed to know their language, as they frolicked side by side.
Of suitors, she had many fair, who came from far and near,
But she'd have none of these, because another she loved dear.

(Photo by Vicki Abbott)

He was the King of Fairies, and he loved her too 'tis
said,
But he a mortal could not marry, so they could
not wed.
The fairies called a meeting to discuss the King's sad
plight,
The sea nymphs came, and all agreed that this should
be made right.
The God of Love presided, and suggestions were
received,
By none the problem would be solved, there everyone
agreed.
"I have it" said the God of Love, and he gave his
head a nod
"We'll make this maid a fairy with the status of a
God."
And thereupon he took his wand made of a piece
of log,

And when he touched her on the head she became a
Maltese dog.
And so they lived there afterwards as happy as
could be, The Fairy King and Melita on this island
in the sea.

★   ★   ★   ★   ★   ★

Ah' this is but a fairy tale and not one word is true,
but you'll believe it after you have read this whole book
through.

Once you have owned a Maltese, there will
never be a question in your mind about why most
Maltese breeders and fanciers are so sentimental
about the breed. There is not another breed so
lovely and so endearing.

(Photo by Crisandra Maltese)

APPENDIX A

Resources

PARENT CLUB AND ORGANIZATIONS

The American Maltese Association, Inc.
www.americanmaltese.org
(Contact the AKC for the current club secretary address.)

AMA Rescue
(Contact the AMA secretary or the AMA Web site for current contact information.)

AMA Education Committee and Illustrated Guide to the Maltese Standard
(Contact the AMA secretary or the AMA Web site for current contact information.)

AMA Heath and Welfare Committee
(Contact the AMA secretary or the AMA Web site for current contact information.)

Kennel Clubs and Registries

The American Kennel Club
5580 Centerview Dr., Suite 200
Raleigh, NC 27606
919-233-9767
www.akc.org

AKC Breeder Referral Service
900-407-7877 (not a free call)

Canadian Kennel Club
Commerce Park
89 Skyway Ave., Suite 100
Etobicoke, Ontario M9W 6R4

United Kennel Club
100 East Kilgore
Kalamazoo, MI 49001-5588
616-343-9020
www.ukedogs.com

Assistance Dog Organizations

Canine Companions for Independence
P.O. Box 446
Santa Rosa, CA 95402-0446
707-577-1790
www.caninecompanions.org

Canine Hearing Companions, Inc.
247 E. Forest Grove Rd.
Vineland, NJ 08360

Delta Society for Pet Partners
289 Perimeter Rd. East
Renton, WA 98055
800-869-6898
www2.deltasociety.org/deltasociety/

Dogs for the Deaf, Inc.
10175 Wheeler Rd.
Central Point, OR 97502
www.dogsforthedeaf.org

Guide Dogs for the Blind
P.O. Box 151200
San Rafael, CA 94015
415-499-4000
www.guidedogs.com

Love on a Leash
P.O. Box 6308
Oceanside, CA 92058
619-724-8878

Therapy Dogs, Inc.
P.O. Box 2786
Cheyenne, WY 82003
307-638-3223
www.home.ptd.net/~compudog/tdi.html

Therapy Dogs International
6 Hilltop Rd.
Mendham, NJ 07945
201-543-0888

Rescue Organizations

AVID Microchip I.D.
800-336–AVID
www.avidplc.com

**HomeAgain, AKC Companion
Animal Recovery**
5580 Centerview Dr., Suite 250
Raleigh, NC 27606-3394
800-252-7894
www.akc.org

National Association for Search and Rescue
4500 Southgate Place, Suite 100
Chantilly, VA 20151-1714
703-222-6277
www.nasar.org

Health and Research

AKC Canine Health Foundation
251 West Garfield Rd., Suite 160
Aurora, OH 44202-8856
330-995-0807
(re: American Maltese Association Donor Advised Fund)

Canine Eye Registration Foundation (CERF)
South Campus Courts, Building C
Purdue University
West Lafayette, IN 47907
317-494-8179
www.vet.purdue.edu/~yshen/cerf.html

Orthopedic Foundation for Animals (OFA)
2300 Nifong Blvd.
Columbia, MO 65201
573-442-0418
www.ofa.org

PennHip/International Canine Genetics
271 Great Valley Pkwy.
Malvern, PA 19355
610-640-1244 or 800-248-8099

Events

American Temperament Test Society
P.O. Box 397
Fenton, MO 63026
314-225-5346

North American Dog Agility Council
HCR 2 Box 277
St. Maries, ID 83861
208-689-3803
www.teleport.com/~jhaglund/nadachom.htm

U.S. Dog Agility Association
P.O. Box 850955
Richardson, TX 75085-0955
972-231-9700
www.usdaa.com

Other

American Dog Owners Association
1654 Columbia Tpk.
Castleton, NY 12033
518-477-8469
www.global2000.net/adoa

(Photo by Pamela G. Rightmyer)

American Maltese Association Code of Ethics

1. As a member of the American Maltese Association (AMA), I will breed to the ideals of the Maltese Standard and will act in accordance to the objectives and purposes of the AMA. I will abide by and uphold the principles of the Club's Constitution and this Code of Ethics.

2. I will keep alert for and endeavor to control or eradicate inherited problems that are particular to my breed. I will strive to screen my breeding stock for hereditary problems.

3. If any of my Maltese need to be euthanized, it will be done in a most humane manner by a veterinarian. It will not be done at a dog pound, humane society, or experimental lab, nor will they be left alive at any of these places.

4. I will provide adequate diet and exercise, and veterinary care and supervision during gestation, whelping, and lactation.

5. I will not knowingly deal with dog wholesalers, retailers, or unethical dog breeders, nor supply dogs for raffles, "give away" prizes, or other such projects.

(Photo by Andrea Noel)

6. I will keep accurate breeding and stud records as required by AKC.

7. My puppies will receive quality health care and nutrition. They will be handled regularly, properly socialized, and accustomed to human contact.

8. I will not sell a puppy before it has been given a veterinarian health examination and has received at least one inoculation against distemper, hepatitis, and parvo. A puppy will remain in my possession until at least 12 weeks of age.

9. I will provide pet buyers with written details on feeding, general care and nutrition and a health record with data on veterinary attention.

10. I will provide limited registration on puppies sold as pets or have signed spay/neuter agreements.

11. I will not speak with dishonor of another member or seek to impair the reputation of another breeder. I will be courteous and helpful to people who contact me regarding dog information.

12. While staying in a hotel/motel during Specialty shows and all-breed shows, I will obey the rules, regulations and policies pertaining to dogs. Upon proof of violations, I assume the risk of suspension from the AMA with a letter of grievance filed with AKC recommending disciplinary action.

13. I understand that failure to comply with the Code of Ethics will subject me to possible suspension or expulsion from the AMA.

Adopted July 1995

(Photo by Sandra Kenner & Christine Pearson)

Titles a Maltese Can Earn

AMERICAN KENNEL CLUB TITLES

Conformation and Dual Titles

Championship titles always precede the dog's name.

Ch.	Conformation Champion of Record
DC or Dual Ch.	Conformation and Field Champion
TC	Triple Champion (CH, FC and OTCh)
CT	Champion Tracker

Obedience Titles

Titles for obedience and other performance events come after the name of the dog.

CD	Companion Dog
CDX	Companion Dog Excellent

UD	Utility Dog
UDX	Utility Dog Excellent
OTCh.	Obedience Trial Champion

Field Titles

FC	Field Champion
AFC	Amateur Field Champion
FC/AFC	FC and AFC
JH	Junior Hunter
SH	Senior Hunter
MH	Master Hunter

Tracking Titles

TD	Tracking Dog
TDX	Tracking Dog Excellent
VST	Variable Surface Tracking Dog

Combination Titles

UDT	Utility Dog Tracker
UDTX	Utility Dog Tracker Excellent

Agility Titles

NA	Novice Agility
OA	Open Agility
AX	Agility Excellent
MX	Master Agility

Canine Good Citizen

The Canine Good Citizen title, although sponsored by The American Kennel Club, is not officially recognized on an AKC pedigree. Most owners with a dog that has achieved this unofficial title will put it after the name of the dog: CGC, or Canine Good Citizen.

AMA Titles

The American Maltese Association gives the title of ROM, or Register of Merit, to a dog or bitch that is a top producer. To qualify for this title, a dog must have sired at least five AKC Champions of record, and a bitch must be the dam of three or more AKC Champions of Record. The ROM title is placed after the name of the dog and is not one of the official titles recognized by the AKC.

United Kennel Club Titles

UKC titles precede the name of the dog.

U-Ch.	Champion
U-CD	Companion Dog
U-CDX	Companion Dog Excellent
U-UD	Utility Dog
HR	Hunting Retriever
HR Ch.	Hunting Retriever Champion
GRHR Ch.	Grand Hunting Retriever Champion
U-AGI	Agility One (Novice)
U-AGII	Agility Two (Advanced)
U-Ach.	Agility Champion

CKC Titles

Most Canadian Kennel Club titles are the same as those used by the AKC, except:

OTCh.	The same as an AKC Utility Dog
FTCh.	Field Trial Champion
AFTCh.	Amateur Field Trial Champion
WC	Working Certificate
WCI	Working Certificate Intermediate
WCX	Working Certificate Excellent
ADC	Agility Dog of Canada
AADC	Advanced Agility Dog of Canada
MADC	Master Agility Dog of Canada

NADAC Titles

NAC	Novice Agility Certificate
OAC	Open Agility Certificate
EAC	Elite Agility Certificate
NATCh.	NADAC Agility Champion

North American Dog Agility Council titles are also available for different classes, such as Gamblers and Jumpers. These would be NGC, OGC, EGC and so on.

United States Dog Agility Association Titles

Ad	Agility Dog
AAD	Advanced Agility Dog
MAD	Master Agility Dog
JM	Jumpers Master Dog
GM	Gamblers Master Dog
SM	Snooker Master Dog
RM	Relay Master Dog
VAD	Veteran Agility Dog
ADCh.	Agility Dog Champion

Other Titles

TD	Therapy Dog
TDI	Therapy Dog International
TT	Temperament Test of the ATTS
SKC Ch.	States Kennel Club Champion
UCI Int. Ch.	International Champion, earned in the United States
Int. Ch.	International Champion

Common Abbreviations

BIS	Best in Show
BOB	Best of Breed
BOS	Best of Opposite Sex
BISS	Best in Specialty Show
WD	Winners Dog
WB	Winners Bitch
BW	Best of Winners
RWD	Reserve Winners Dog
RWB	Reserve Winners Bitch
HIT	High in Trial
HC	High Combined (from Open and Utility obedience classes)

(Photo by Alverson Photographers)

A P P E N D I X D

American Maltese Association National Specialty Winners

First National Specialty

June 11, 1966
Salem, Ohio
BOB—Ch. Co-Ca-He's Aennchen's Toy Dancer
Owner/Handler: Anna Marie Stimmler

Second National Specialty

June 24–25, 1967
Beverly Hills, California
BOB—Ch. Aennchen's Poona Dancer
Breeder: Aennchen Antonelli
Owner: Frank Oberstar and Larry Ward
Handler: Frank Oberstar

Third National Specialty

March 30, 1968
Pittsburgh, Pennsylvania
BOB—Ch. Aennchen's Poona Dancer
Breeder: Aennchen Antonelli
Owner: Frank Oberstar and Larry Ward
Handler: Frank Oberstar

Fourth National Specialty

April 5–6, 1969
Chicago, Illinois
BOB—Ch. Pendleton's Jewel
Breeder: Anne Pendleton
Owner/Handler: Dottie White

Fifth National Specialty

July 26, 1970
Santa Barbara, California
BOB—Ch. Pendleton's Jewel
Breeder: Anne Pendleton
Owner/Handler: Dottie White

Sixth National Specialty (First Independent Specialty)

February 14, 1971
New York, New York
BOB—Ch. Pendleton's Jewel
Breeder: Anne Pendleton
Owner/Handler: Dottie White

Seventh National Specialty

April 1–2, 1972
Chicago, Illinois
BOB—Ch. Joanne-Chen's Maya Dancer
Breeder: Joanne Hesse
Owner: Joe and Mamie Gregory
Handler: Peggy Hogg

Eighth National Specialty

August 4–5, 1973
Seattle, Washington
BOB—Ch. Mike-Mar's Sirius of Revlo
Breeder: Mike Wolf
Owner: Mary Olver
Handler: Elaine Mitchell

Ninth National Specialty

January 19, 1974
Hileah, Florida
BOB—Ch. Cara Maya's Mister
Owner: Shirley Hrabak

Tenth National Specialty

March 7, 1975
Detroit, Michigan
BOB—Ch. Celia's Mooney Forget Me Not
Owner: Priscilla Brown and Lara Olive
Handler: Priscilla Brown

Eleventh National Specialty

April 3, 1976
Las Vegas, Nevada
BOB—Ch. So Big's Desert Delight
Owner: Freda Tinsley
Handler: Rebecca Tinsley

Twelfth National Specialty

September 4, 1977
Elizabeth, New Jersey
BOB—Ch. Oak Ridge Country Charmer
Breeder/Owner: Carol and Tom Neth
Handler: Carol Neth

Thirteenth National Specialty

September 6, 1978
Houston, Texas
BOB—Ch. Su-Le's Jonina
Breeder/Owner: Barbara Bergquist
Handler: Annette Lurton

Fourteenth National Specialty

September 15, 1979
San Mateo, California
BOB—Ch. Oak Ridge Country Charmer
Breeder/Owner: Carol and Tom Neth
Handler: Carol Neth

Fifteenth National Specialty

July 9, 1980
North Hampton, Massachussetts
BOB—Ch. Joanne-Chen's Mino Maya Dancer
Breeder: Joanne Hesse
Owner: Blanche Tenerowicz
Handler: Daryl Martin

Sixteenth National Specialty

August 5, 1981
Houston, Texas
BOB—Ch. Joanne-Chen's Mino Maya Dancer
Breeder: Joanne Hesse
Owner: Blanche Tenerowicz
Handler: Daryl Martin

Seventeenth National Specialty

October 23, 1982
Las Vegas Nevada
BOB—Ch. Rebecca's Desert Valentino
Breeder/Owner: Freda Tinsley
Handler: Don Rodgers

Eighteenth National Specialty

June 3, 1983
Natick, Massachussetts
BOB—Ch. Nobel Faith's White Tornado
Breeder/Owner: Faith Knobel
Handler: Barbara Alderman

Nineteenth National Specialty

May 4, 1984
Madison, Wisconsin
BOB—Ch. Myi's Ode to Glory Seeker
Breeder/Owner: Beverly Passe
Handler: Peggy Hogg

Twentieth National Specialty

May 23, 1985
Claremont, California
BOB—Ch. Non-Vel's Weejun
Breeder: Helen Hood
Owner: Candes Mathes and Mary Senkowski
Handler: Bill Cunningham

Twenty-First National Specialty

June 19, 1986
Orlando, Florida
BOB—Ch. Villa Malta's Chicklett
Breeder: Marge Rozik
Owner: Tom and Nancy Jennings
Handler: Joylynn Woodard

Twenty-Second National Specialty

June 3–4, 1987
Elk Grove, Illinois
BOB—Ch. Bar-None Electric Horseman
Breeder: Michelle Perlmutter
Owner: Jackie and Keith Garber
Handler: Augustin Gomez

Twenty-Third National Specialty

October 27–28, 1988
Phoenix, Arizona
BOB—Ch. C and M's Tootsey's Lollypop
Breeder: Mary Day and Carol Thomas
Owner: Sherry Lemond Ray, Mary Day and Carol Thomas
Handler: Mary Day

Twenty-Fourth National Specialty

October 27–28, 1989
Parsippany, New Jersey
BOB—Ch. Two Be's Hooked on Sugar
Breeder/Owner: Betty Eaton and Billie Edwards
Handler: Pat Keen

Twenty-Fifth National Specialty (Silver Anniversary Specialty)

August 21–22, 1990
North Randall, Ohio
BOB—Ch. Sand Island Small Kraft Lite
Breeder/Owner: Carol Frances Andersen
Handler: Vicki Abbott

Twenty-Sixth National Specialty

June 6–7, 1991
Tacoma, Washington
BOB—Ch. Sand Island Small Kraft Lite
Breeder/Owner: Carol Frances Andersen
Handler: Vicki Abbott

Twenty-Seventh National Specialty

August 1–2, 1992
Ft. Lauderdale, Florida
BOB—Ch. C and M's Tootsey's Lollypop
Breeder: Mary Day and Carole Thomas
Owner: Sherry Lemond Ray, Mary Day and
Carole Thomas
Handler: Mary Day

Twenty-Eighth National Specialty

September 30–October 1, 1993
Southgate, Michigan
BOB—Ch. Melodylane Sings O' Al-Mar Luv
Breeder: Marjorie Lewis
Owner: Mariko Sukezaki and David and Sharon
Newcomb
Handler: Vicki Abbott

Twenty-Ninth National Specialty

May 19–20, 1994
Del Mar, California
BOB—Ch. Shanlyn's Rais'n A Raucous
Breeder: Lynda Podgurski
Owner: Joseph Joly III, Vicki Abbott and David
and Sharon Newcomb
Handler: Vicki Abbott

Thirtieth National Specialty

July 4–5, 1995
West Springfield, Massachussetts
BOB—Ch. Merri Paloma

Breeder/Owner: Barbara Merrick and David
Fitzpatrick
Handler: Jason Hoke

Thirty-First National Specialty

April 11–12, 1996
Minneapolis, Minnesota
BOB—Ch. Ta-Jon's Tickle Me Silly
Breeder/Owner: Tammy and John Simon
Handler: Tammy Simon

Thirty-Second National Specialty

July 15–16, 1997
Millbrae, California
BOB—Ch. Ta-Jon's Tickle Me Silly
Breeder: Tammy and John Simon
Owner: Samuel and Marion Lawrence
Handler: Tammy Simon

Thirty-Third National Specialty

August 19–21, 1998
Harrisburg, Pennsylvania
BOB—Ch. Marcris Risque Omen
Breeder/Owner: Joyce Watkins
Handler: Barbara Cantlon

Thirty-Fourth National Specialty

May 27–28, 1999
New Orleans, Louisiana
BOB—Ch. Showboat Miss Piggy of C and M
Breeder: Barbara Brown
Owner: Barbara Brown and Peter J. Rogers III
Handler: Peter J. Rogers III

Bibliography

BOOKS

About Maltese

Abbott, Vicki. *A New Owner's Guide to Maltese*. Neptune City, NJ: TFH Publications, 1997.

Antonelli, J. P. *The Maltese Scrapbook*. Pittsburgh, PA: Dorrance Publishing Company, 1998.

Berndt, Robert J. *Your Maltese*. Fairfax, VA: Denlinger's, 1975.

Brearly, Joan McDonald. *The Book of the Maltese*. Neptune City, NJ: TFH Publications, 1984.

Cutillo, Nicholas. *The Complete Maltese*. New York: Howell Book House, 1986.

Herrieff, Vicki. *The Maltese Today*. Lydney, Gloucestershire, UK: Ringpress Books Ltd., 1996.

Nicholas, Anna Katherine. *The Maltese*. Neptune City, NJ: TFH Publications, 1984.

About Showing and Training

Alston, George G., with Connie Vanacore. *The Winning Edge: Show Ring Secrets*. New York: Howell Book House, 1992.

Bauman, Diane. *Beyond Basic Dog Training*. New York: Howell Book House, 1986.

Forsyth, Jane, and Robert Forsyth. *The Forsyth Guide to Successful Dog Showing*. New York: Howell Book House, 1976.

Johnson, Glen. *Tracking Dog, Theory and Methods*. Westmoreland, NY: Arner Publications, 1975.

Morsell, Curt. *Training Your Dog to Win Obedience Titles*. New York: Howell Book House, 1976.

Simmons-Moake, Jane. *Agility Training: The Fun Sport For All Dogs*. New York: Howell Book House, 1991.

Volhard, Joachim, and Gail Fischer. *Training Your Dog: A Step By Step Manual*. New York: Howell Book House, 1984.

About the Structure of the Dog

Elliot, Rachel Page. *The New Dogsteps*. New York: Howell Book House, 1983.

Lyon, McDowell. *The Dog in Action*. New York: Howell Book House, 1978.

About Behavior and Health

Carlson, D.G., DVM, and James M. Giffin, MD. *Dog Owner's Home Veterinary Handbook*. New York: Howell Book House, 1994.

Dunbar, Ian, Ph.D., MRCUS. *Dog Behavior: An Owner's Guide to a Happy, Healthy Pet*. New York: Howell Book House, 1998.

Evans, J.M. and Kay White. *The Doglopaedia: A Complete Guide to Dog Care*. New York: Howell Book House, 1997.

Fogle, Bruce, DVM, MRCUS. *The Dog's Mind*. New York: Howell Book House, 1990.

The Monks of New Skete. *How to Be Your Dog's Best Friend*. Boston: Little, Brown and Co., 1978.

Petersen, David E. *Dog and Cat Longevity*. Bloomington, MN: Pet Life Extension Associates, 1993.

Pitcairn, Richard H., DVM, and Susan Hubble Pitcairn. *Dr. Pitcairn's Complete Guide to Natural Health for Dogs & Cats*. Emmaus, PA: Rodale Press, 1982.

Rutherford, Clarice, and David Neil. *How to Raise a Puppy You Can Live With*. Loveland, CO: Alpine Publications, 1981.

About Breeding

Hansen, Joseph S., VMD. *How To Breed and Whelp Dogs*. Springfield, IL: Charles C. Thomas Publishing, 1972.

Harmar, Hilary. *Dogs and How To Breed Them*. London: John Gifford Ltd., 1974.

Hutt, Frederick B, DVM. *Genetics for Dog Breeders*. San Francisco: W. H. Freeman and Co., 1979.

Seranne, Ann. *The Joy of Breeding Your Own Show Dog*. New York: Howell Book House, 1981.

About Travel with Your Dog

ASPCA. *Traveling with Your Pet*. ASPCA Ed. Dept., 441 E. 92nd St., New York, NY 10128.

Gaines Pet Food Corp. *Touring with Bowser*. Gaines, P.O. Box 5700, Kankakee, IL 60902.

General Reference About Dogs

American Kennel Club. *The Complete Dog Book, 19th Edition Revised*. New York: Howell Book House, 1998.

Jones, Arthur F., and Ferelith Hamilton. *The World Encyclopedia of Dogs*. New York: Galahad Books, 1971.

Taylor, David. *The Ultimate Dog Book*. New York: Simon and Schuster, 1990.

PERIODICALS

The Maltese Rx
This national publication put out by the American Maltese Association is available by subscription. Contact the AMA at their Web site, www.americanmaltese.org, for the current editor or corresponding secretary.

The Maltese Magazine
P.O. Box 6369
Los Osos, CA, 93412

AKC Gazette and Events Calendar
5580 Centerview Drive
Raleigh, NC 27609-0643
919-233-9727

Top Knotch Toys Magazine
8848 Beverly Hills
Lakeland, FL 33809

EDUCATIONAL MATERIALS ON THE MALTESE STANDARD

The Illustrated Guide to the Maltese Standard
This publication is put out by the parent club and can be ordered by contacting the Education chairperson. You can obtain that information from the AMA Web site or from the AKC.

The Official AKC Maltese Video
5580 Centerview Drive
Raleigh, NC 27609-0643
919-233-9767

Index